PRAISE FOR **BETTER OFF** with*out* **JESUS**

How do we know when it's the Spirit or just our emotions? We have all made foolish decisions by mistaking our feelings for God's leading. Those decisions often lead to pain and regret. My friend Chuck does a great job of explaining the process of joining Scripture with the Spirit's leading in order to honor Christ in our decisions. This is a much needed tool in a time when so many lack discernment.

Francis Chan
Bestselling Author of *Crazy Love* and *Forgotten God*

For Chuck, "spirituality" is not about life in another world but about God's living presence at work right in the middle of this one. I found *Better Off Without Jesus* to be profound, refreshing and inspiring.

John Mark Comer
Author of *My Name Is Hope: Anxiety, Depression and Life After Melancholy*
Lead Pastor of Solid Rock, Portland, Oregon

I've known Chuck for several years, and it's obvious that he has not written this book to make a name for himself but to pastor people into a more vibrant and intimate relationship with Jesus. Chuck's candid vulnerability will leave you disarmed and intrigued as he clearly and fervently calls you to a more passionate and humble encounter with the Holy Spirit. This book did not leave me with the desire to know "about" the Holy Spirit; it made me want to get on my hands and knees and experience Him personally.

Mike Donehey
Lead Singer of Tenth Avenue North

How do we know what God is telling us to do? Sometimes we make it awkward or mysterious, but in *Better Off Without Jesus*, Chuck Bomar makes it street-level practical by letting us into his own experience of trying to figure out the right next steps for situations in his life.

Reggie Joiner
Founder and CEO of Orange

Chuck brings practical truth and insight to what is often a neglected and confusing part of the Christian life. I firmly believe that if we would practice what Chuck writes about in this book our lives—and thus our churches—we would be incredibly changed.

Dan Kimball
Author of *They Like Jesus but Not the Church*
Pastor of Vintage Faith Church, Santa Cruz, California

Better Off Without Jesus helps those of us who never know what to say when someone tells us, "God told me . . ." Chuck brings the issues of spiritual living and biblical discernment into the adventure of living in the Kingdom in a way that moves people toward a deeper spirituality as they follow Jesus.

Rick McKinley
Author of *This Beautiful Mess* and *A Kingdom Called Desire*

Raw, honest, piercing, insightful. There's not a human on the planet who doesn't wrestle with how to communicate with a God you can't see yet can know as the realest being in the universe. Chuck sees God in the ordinary and mundane, in the trenches of everyday life, and he calls us to a faith that is about faithfulness. I suppose that every person who reads this book will respond differently to it. For me, it was a trip down memory lane in the life of a friend. I have seen how God has made theological truths—truth we tend to talk a lot about in the fiery furnace of life—experientially real in Chuck, a man I love and respect.

Todd Nighswonger
Senior Pastor of Cornerstone Community Church, Simi Valley, California

Someone once described Pentecost as a party. The coming of the Holy Spirit is the birthday of the Church. But, sadly, the Church has forgotten how to dance. By God's grace, Christians are boldly re-engaging the life of the Spirit in the Church and the world. Thankfully, we've got a friend like Chuck to lead the way. Chuck actually believes the words on these pages, and he tries to live them as well. That's why I love this book, and why you will love it as well. If living by the Spirit is a party, then *Better Off Without Jesus* reminds us we're invited to the dance.

A. J. Swoboda, Ph.D.
Professor, Pastor and Author of *Messy: God Likes It That Way*

BETTER OFF without JESUS

"It is to your advantage that I go away"

JESUS

BETTER OFF without JESUS

CHUCK BOMAR

Regal

For more information and
special offers from Regal Books, email us at
subscribe@regalbooks.com

Published by Regal
From Gospel Light
Ventura, California, U.S.A.
www.regalbooks.com
Printed in the U.S.A.

Library of Congress Cataloging-in-Publication Data
Bomar, Chuck.
Better off without Jesus / Chuck Bomar.
p. cm.
ISBN 978-0-8307-6411-2 (trade paper)
1. Holy Spirit. 2. Jesus Christ—Presence. I. Title.
BT123.B66 2012
231'.3—dc23
2012013622

Rights for publishing this book outside the U.S.A. or in non-English languages
are administered by Gospel Light Worldwide, an international not-for-profit ministry.
For additional information, please visit www.glww.org, email info@glww.org, or write
to Gospel Light Worldwide, 1957 Eastman Avenue, Ventura, CA 93003, U.S.A.

To order copies of this book and other Regal products in bulk quantities,
please contact us at 1-800-446-7735.

DEDICATION

This book is dedicated to my beautiful wife, Barbara, who has walked with me and supported me through thick and thin. I can't think of a better "biggest fan"! I am so thankful for your support, grace and consistent unconditional love.

Oh, and Karis, Hope and Sayla . . . your daddy loves you more than you can ever imagine.

CONTENTS

CHAPTER 1

Why Physical Presence
Isn't Always Best

"Better off *without* Jesus."

I know, some things just don't seem right at first. But that doesn't mean they're wrong.

Sometimes it's just a matter of perspective.

In November 2007, I made the decision to plant a church in Portland, Oregon. I had been serving at a fantastic church in Southern California for about eight-and-a-half years. But it was time to move on.

Most people were excited for me, including the elders of our church, but there were a few people who thought it didn't seem right.

"Why would you leave?" they asked. This was a great church where I had longevity, a great ministry; and I was loved and cared for better than anyone on a church staff needs to be. We had a "steady paycheck," a great group of friends and people I was personally investing in one on one.

Because of these things, some people thought I was a complete idiot to leave. They could not see how this could possibly be beneficial for me, for my family or for the ministries I was leading. When I told them we were not going to ask for funding from our church or try to raise funds from outside sources, some began to *really* question my steps of action.

We were planting a church in an "unorthodox" way, and it just so happened to be during the worst recession anyone alive had seen. Some people told me I was being erratic, irresponsible and unwise; and one man even said I was being selfish, suggesting that I was putting my family at risk for an "adrenaline rush." My daughters were three years old and four months old at the time, and here I was moving a thousand miles away to an area I knew little about, and with no job and no funding.

And I didn't even have a mission statement for the church.

I had no personal friends in the area and barely knew two of my wife's friends from college who lived there. We didn't have any family in the area. In fact, my wife's mother had cancer at the time and, once we moved, wouldn't be able to come and visit. It was too far to drive, and she wasn't allowed to fly. Making a decision to move away from your family is one thing; but taking your wife away from hers is another.

A lot of circumstances didn't add up, I guess, but they don't necessarily need to for something to be right. When God calls you to go somewhere, you just go.

In every step of faith there are a lot of unanswered questions, and there are always things that don't seem right to those outside of the decision—and at times even to us taking the steps. But those of us who are seeking to take steps of obedience always experience peace when we do so. We ask different questions than others around us. And by seeking God's direction and following it, we become more and more confident in our ability to hear God speak.

Hearing God is what this book is about helping you do. If I can help you become more confident in your ability to hear God's voice, this book is a success for me.

The bottom line is that my wife and I were totally confident that this was a step of faith God was telling us to take. So in April

2008, we packed our things and parachuted into Portland to plant Colossae Church.

People have asked me how I knew God was calling me to move to Portland, or how I knew for sure I was supposed to plant a church versus do something else. To help answer that it will be helpful for you to first understand a few things that God has brought me through. I need to fill you in on some trials I've faced and sins I've committed. With that knowledge, I believe you will see how all of it has led to my being able to more accurately decipher God's voice.

Preferred Comfort in the Physical

First, let me just say that, as a Christian, I hold the conviction that the most reverent thing we can do is take Jesus' words seriously, process them and then let them practically drive every aspect of our lives. To not take this approach would be irreverent.

If you agree, let's dive into the words of Jesus:

Jesus says to His disciples, "Nevertheless, I tell you the truth: it is to your advantage that I go away, for if I do not go away, the Helper will not come to you. But if I go, I will send him to you" (John 16:7).

These are powerful words; and as confused as the disciples seemed to be by them, Jesus had plenty of reason to make such a statement.

By the time we get to this verse in the Gospel of John, Jesus has been talking with His disciples for two chapters about His soon-to-come departure. They had been trying to wrap their minds around this idea but were having a very difficult time doing so. They had left everything to follow Jesus, and now He's telling them they're better off without Him.

The fact that Jesus makes this statement leads us to assume it's true. But there are some questions that arise as we process it further. For starters, how could this possibly be *better* for His disciples?

Simple, I guess. If we look back at the verse from a 30,000-foot perspective, the answer is that Jesus has to leave *so that* the Helper will come. He also words it in the negative, saying that if He doesn't leave, the Helper will not come.

Okay, that may be clear, but why is *that* better?

How could His leaving possibly put His disciples into a more advantageous situation?

Clearly, they were not comfortable with this idea; and as we read this section of Scripture, they obviously didn't fully grasp what was happening.

It seems like, if anything, they would easily get off track and lose focus without Him. Up to this point, there was a lot they didn't understand. They had a hard enough time deciphering the difference between right and wrong with Jesus by their side. Time after time they had questions or didn't get what was happening, so they were always looking to Jesus' example, fully reliant on Him to keep their thinking straight, and asking Him questions so that things would be clear.

For instance, in Mark 4, we see Jesus teaching people from a boat while they stood on the shore of the Sea of Galilee. He had stepped into a boat because the crowd was mobbing Him while on land. At this point, He had been healing people and doing all sorts of miracles that had attracted massive crowds. So He created a little separation from them by getting into a boat and pushing out a bit before teaching again. As part of this teaching, He told a parable about a sower (see Mark 4:3-9).

There was deep meaning to be found in this parable, and most of the listeners probably knew it but they couldn't figure out the meaning. Most of them got nothing more out of it than a story about a farmer. They left confused.

But the disciples had a huge advantage over the crowd. Afterward, when they were alone with Jesus, the 12 disciples asked Him to explain the parable so they could understand. And so, Jesus explained it further (see Mark 4:10-20).

I don't know about you, but having Jesus explain His teaching seems like it would be pretty helpful. How could the *Helper* possibly provide more practical help than that? His voice was their norm. It was what they were used to, and I'm sure they found great comfort in this luxury.

Think about it: It would be physical, immediate, concrete and something they knew how to function with. As human beings, we like these types of situations. We are comfortable in circumstances like this, and for many of us the idea of having an immaterial Helper is tough to wrap our mind around. It's much easier to ask someone standing in front of you to give you an answer.

Because they were so used to the physical presence of Jesus, the promise of the coming Helper must have seemed awfully ambiguous. This is probably, at least in part, why Jesus' disciples were filled with sorrow and confusion when He told them He would be departing (see John 16:22).

Jesus personally counseled them.

He comforted them.

He answered their questions.

He clarified misunderstandings.

He guided them.

He let them know when they were off base.

I've often found myself reading the Bible, looking at different situations with Jesus, and thinking of what it would have been like to be one of the disciples. I try to picture myself walking with Jesus along the Sea of Galilee, or following Him as He turns over money tables and casts out demons in the synagogue, heals people, calms storms or eats with the outcasts of society. To walk alongside Him as He made His way through the crowds would be amazing and certainly helpful to learn from.

Oh, to be able to ask a question and then have Him answer it immediately! That seems like the best possible scenario. And to be frank, when I read passages like Mark 4:34, I get a little envious of the disciples. It says that Jesus spoke in parables, "but privately to his own disciples he explained everything."

That seems "practical" to me. In contrast, most of us, if we are honest, think that following the Holy Spirit seems ambiguous and possibly overly subjective.

How do we know it's Him speaking?

With Jesus physically by our side, we would at least know it was Him.

So, What Do I Do Now?

I find that most of us, when we think about it, truly believe that we would be better off with Jesus by our side. We desperately want to do what God wants; we want to be where He wants us to be, and we tirelessly pursue this clarity. We want God to speak, and we want Him to do so in ways that are undoubtedly Him. We don't want to be left guessing in the land of ambiguity. We want full assurance.

One night in the summer of 2005, I remember lying facedown in my living room, crying out to God for answers. I desperately needed to hear from Him. Earlier that day, I was put in an extremely difficult situation that ended up changing the course of my life. I was praying and reading Scripture fervently, hoping something would just *pop* out.

I have never heard God's audible voice, but if there was ever a time when I wanted Him to show up in this way, this was it. I needed God to say something. Anything.

I remember literally saying out loud, "Jesus, I just wish You were here so You could tell me what to do."

I'll be filling you in much more on this situation in the coming pages, but it's in times of desperation that we most earnestly seek God's counsel. And as physical creatures, we often long for the intimate and physical presence of Jesus to bring the clarity that we desire.

But, our pursuit for clarity from God is not just in moments of desperation. We ask God to guide us through all sorts of circumstances and even in some of the most monotonous situations.

What college do I go to?

What school do I send my child to?

Do we apply for loans or work our way through school?

Which house do I buy . . . and where?

Which job does God want me to have?

Should I buy a car?

Do I spank my children or give timeouts?

I have totally pure motives; so I don't understand why God isn't . . . (you finish the sentence).

These are all examples of situations in which we genuinely want to be in tune with God. And, again, many of us think we would be better off with Jesus right by our side. We like the idea of being able to ask Him questions about our lives whenever we want to. It's comforting and physical and immediate. As relational beings, we're used to it like this.

And yet, this is where we need to take our first full step back and honestly examine the reasons why we think this way.

The reality is that we assume it would be best for Jesus to be physically beside us because we are focused on ourselves. Unfortunately, it's usually at the expense of keeping in mind all that God is also doing in the lives of other people, and around the world.

When I cried out that night on my living room floor, wishing that Jesus was by my side, I was only thinking about myself. I wasn't concerned about everything God was doing beyond me. I had my own problems.

I wanted to do what God wanted me to do, and I had decisions to make.

But there was more that was feeding my thinking—much more than I would like to admit.

The culture we live in breeds individualism deep into the core of our being. We lose sight of others and become mostly concerned about ourselves, our questions, our families, our pursuits, our decisions, our responsibilities. In fact, I've noticed that most people who have grown up and live in our Western culture don't believe their lives can actually be focused on serving others. They have too many things going on in their own lives.

This unawareness of how much our culture drives our thinking toward individualistic thoughts is perhaps the biggest hindrance to hearing God speak to us.

One of the biggest lessons I've learned is that focusing on myself actually muffles the voice of God right out of my life.

Our Western culture would lead us to embrace Jesus solely as a beneficial addition to *our* individual lives, goals and dreams. We think we need to invite Him to join every area of *our* lives. But the truth is that He calls us to join in with His.

Understanding this difference is absolutely essential if you want to be in tune with God's voice in your life. If you want to hear God speak to you individually, you must begin thinking beyond yourself.

The Bigger Picture

Jesus had a much bigger picture in mind for His followers than how they benefited individually. Sure, He cared about them individually, and He cares about every one of us individually; and we certainly do have eternal benefits because of all He accomplished (see Eph. 2:4-10). But, to grasp what Jesus is getting at with His statement in John 16:7 about sending the Helper after He leaves, we have to look beyond ourselves.

As we look into the Scriptures, it is abundantly clear that our coming to faith isn't just for personal gain. It's not to make our lives better, but instead to make the excellencies of God known (see 1 Pet. 2:9-10). We benefit greatly because of what Jesus did for us, but understanding this is what pushes us to think and live beyond ourselves (see 2 Cor. 5:14-15).

This truth can be tough to reconcile in our minds, but there is a major distinction we need to make before going any further. If our goal is to serve ourselves and make sure that all of our personal questions get answered in the timeframe we want them answered, then it would be more advantageous to have Jesus physically at our dinner table. And we might as well ask Jesus to show up through a miraculous visitation whenever we personally have unanswered questions.

However, if our goal is to truly follow through with what the Bible teaches about the Christian life, then we must embrace Jesus' statement that we are better off without Him.

The power of Jesus' promise comes in when we realize Jesus' limitations as a human being.

The Bible is clear that Jesus was God in the flesh (see John 1:14). He was the ultimate paradox of divine God and mortal human. But let's not forget that He was, in fact, a human being. Most of the time when we talk about Jesus, we tend to err on the side of talking exclusively about His divinity (the fact that He was God). In fact, talking about His humanity tends to make us feel a bit uneasy. We are fearful of crossing the line into irreverence and somehow think talking too much about the realities of His human life is dangerous territory.

But talking about Jesus' humanity can actually be an expression of our reverence. He was a human being with limitations, and it's not irreverent to notice or discuss these things. This is a critical part of the story of God—how the gospel applies to our lives and how God is reconciling all things to Himself (see Col. 1:19-20).

Understanding His humanity is critical to understanding the everyday practicality of listening to our Helper.

Jesus was obviously not just merely human; but make no mistake, He was a real person. He was raised in a family with four brothers and two sisters, a mom and a stepdad. He lived and had a home in Capernaum (see Mark 2:1; 3:20). He grew up learning the trade of His earthly father and, most likely, had a job as a carpenter—as any normal boy would have done in that culture. Despite His being sought after by the crowds for all the supernatural things He was doing throughout His ministry, He was also simply known as Mary's son and the son of the carpenter to those who watched Him grow up (see Mark 6:3).

He was just "the boy next door" to a lot of people.

One of Jesus' human restrictions was that He could only be in one place at any given time. He was limited. This meant He could only walk alongside a few people and, therefore, could only personally impact and provide guidance to a limited number. That is, He could only do that while He was here in a physical body.

Jesus knew of His limited capacity, and therefore He knew what was best.

He had to leave. Every one of His followers was better off without Him.

His departure meant the Holy Spirit was now going to come. Why was this better?

Well, one reason is that the Holy Spirit is not limited by having a fleshly body. He can be in every location at any given time (see Ps. 139:7). Jesus walked alongside a few followers, but the Holy Spirit could dwell inside and comfort, guide, help and work through many (see Rom. 8:11). All at the same time.

And this, my friend, is far better for all of us! It's in keeping this bigger picture in mind that we can begin to embrace the reality of our Helper. Every Christian around the world desperately needs the Helper to guide, comfort and direct him or her.

Any individual can think it's better for Jesus to be by *his or her* side. But that's losing sight of the fact that others need His help too.

You see, Jesus always intended to leave His followers to continue the work He started (see John 13:15). For example, in Mark 3:14-15 we see that Jesus gathered His disciples so that they could be with Him (to learn), and then He was going to send them out to teach others. In fact, at the end of Matthew's gospel, Jesus tells His disciples to go into all nations to do this (see Matt. 28:18-20). In other words, He scattered them for the purpose of taking His message to all the world.

That was always the plan, and it remains the plan today. And even though Jesus' leaving them didn't make them feel better or even seem right to them at the time, the physical limitations of Jesus makes His physical presence ultimately unfavorable. If He had remained in His physical human state, His followers would have been alone and without help as they scattered to take the gospel to the whole world.

So, it now becomes practical as to why His disciples are better off without Him. Those followers were now actively joining in the mission they left everything to be a part of. Their concern was now to further the truth about Jesus in all different parts of the world; and each of them, individually, needed the Helper to be inside of him to do this.

It was a bit more of an ambiguous experience than they were used to. Far less immediate and comfortable, I'm sure. And, like us, they now had to try to figure out how to follow and keep in step with the Helper inside of them as they sought to fulfill the mission they were sent on.

Beyond Theory

Over the past 18 years of being a Christian, I have had the privilege of investing in people who have moved to places all over the world as missionaries. A couple of them pastor different churches in the

United States; others have gone to places like Europe, Africa, Indonesia or Papua New Guinea. Could you imagine if they were all dependent upon me being physically alongside them for help?

I'm not trying to compare myself to Jesus in all ways, but my physical limitations certainly can be compared to His. There is no possible way I could physically help all those people in their ministries. And there is no possible way Jesus could do it today in physical form. Which is why we are better off without Him.

Most of us won't be going to a tribe in Papua New Guinea to translate the Bible into a language that has yet to be articulated in written form. Rather, we will remain living on our street, working in the same workplace, taking our kids to school and still shopping at the same grocery store, going to the same soccer field, bank and ballet studio. We will continue living where we are and seek to be faithful with where God has us today.

But even though we understand this, and we don't fall into the trap of thinking the mission field is everywhere else but where we live, we still struggle with the idea of hearing God speak to us and knowing for sure it's Him. We get the overall idea of the Holy Spirit (our Helper and Comforter) being within us, but we still find it too ambiguous to practically grasp in our everyday lives.

It's hard to feel His presence.

It's hard to nail down exactly when it's Him speaking . . . and when it's not.

It's one thing if the Bible says something, but what about all those decisions the Bible doesn't speak to directly?

These are the practicalities we all wonder about. Sitting around and talking about the theology of the Holy Spirit can be helpful, but our faith isn't about intellectual assent. We want practical help in following His voice and will for our lives. We want the ambiguity to lessen so that we can move forward faithfully.

This is precisely why this book will stay focused on embracing some very practical realities of the Holy Spirit in your life and walk you through some simple ways that you can be certain God is speaking to you.

You will learn some things about the Holy Spirit throughout, but even those like me, with a master's degree in divinity, know it's one thing to regurgitate information *about* the Holy Spirit, and it's another to embrace Him practically in your life.

Maybe you know a bit about the Holy Spirit and yet struggle with how subjective and ambiguous following Him seems. Maybe the idea about listening to the Holy Spirit is new to you. You want to follow and listen to God, but you struggle with insecurities in your ability to hear Him speak to you.

You're asking, "How do I know, for sure, He is speaking to me?"

Is it a cloud in the sky?

A bumper sticker on a drive-by vehicle?

A kind of inner peace?

A friend who walks up to you after a church service and has a "word" for you?

Maybe you are considering the possibility that God wants you to move on to something else, but you aren't sure how He would clearly show you if it were so.

Maybe you are thinking through finances, where to move or what to do in a specific relationship or job situation. You don't want to play games, and your faith is far more than just a good thing in your life. So you pray, and seek guidance in the Scriptures, and yet you wonder how that practically plays out through the ins and outs of your day.

This is what I hope the coming pages will help you with. Although you can't reduce God's will for your life to a formula; and on this side of eternity, things will often be more unclear than you would like, many of the gray areas of your life, believe it or not, can become more black and white than you thought possible. In fact, I would suggest to you that following the Holy Spirit is far less ambiguous and subjective than most people think.

We just tend to over think how He works, and we tend to concentrate on the wrong things.

As a pastor, I hope to help you apply the reality of the Holy Spirit within you so that you can recognize His beauty, help and comfort—even in the most mundane aspects of your life. As a Christian, I want to join you as you seek to embrace Him and obey His voice through the internal tensions we all face. And as an author, I hope to somehow word things in a way that leads you to understand just how practical being in tune with our Helper can be.

By God's grace, the following pages will serve you in these ways. So, to make this as practical as I possibly can, let me begin by explaining my personal struggle to hear God speak to me after my life had been turned completely upside down. I'll begin by going back to what led up to that night when I cried out for the physical presence of Jesus.

REFLECTION QUESTIONS

1. Prior to reading this chapter, have you ever put much thought into Jesus' statement in John 16:7? If so, how does this chapter compare to your thoughts?

2. How do you think keeping the bigger picture of all that God is doing around the world will (or should) change your prayer life?

3. What is your biggest insecurity when it comes to hearing God speak to you?

CHAPTER 2

Left but Not Abandoned

It was June 2005. Monday afternoon, about 4:30.

I was sitting in my office, leading a staff meeting, when I spun my chair around to check something on my computer. I opened a document that pertained to our conversation, found what I needed and shared the thought with everyone.

Then, I happened to quickly glance at my email inbox.

This is when a hot, sunny afternoon turned dark and as cold as a meat locker. I remember the moment like it was yesterday. I obviously don't recall every thought I had, but I do remember the emotions that exploded within me. I remember feeling my face flush with emotion. "Shocked" couldn't begin to describe what I was feeling. "Horrified" probably creeps toward it, but I think "*shattered*" most clearly articulates my feelings in this moment.

Because my staff was waiting on me, I was trying to swiftly skim through this lengthy email. But the content only allowed me to go so fast. This was a long confessional from a personal friend. I had known him for a few years, at this point, and my wife and I had grown very close to him. We loved him.

Still do, very much.

A lot led up to it, but just over a year prior to receiving this email, my wife and I had partnered with him in a business venture.

We handled aspects of the business, and he handled others. We were excited about this venture for many reasons, but partnering with our friend was certainly one of those.

This email was to inform me of details regarding the loss of all the funds invested into our company. They were gone. He had lost, used or, some might say, stolen every penny. He shared some logistical insights into how he covered up these truths for the past months and how he was now filing for bankruptcy, apparently to separate himself from any legal obligation to pay back the money. However, the email did explain that his personal desire was to repay the entire amount to us. I believe his intentions were sincere.

The total dollar amount lost, used or stolen was $945,000.

Yes, you read that right. And no, this is not embellished. I wish it were. Well, I take that back. I actually don't. This is a critical part of the story God has given me; because of that, I can honestly say I wouldn't change a thing.

I know, that is a very expensive statement. But I can honestly say I wouldn't change it.

Back to my office . . .

My staff was still sitting in a semicircle, now to my back, as I finished reading the email. With eyes closed and chin on my chest, I took a couple of deep breaths. When I felt like I could at least utter a few words, I slowly rotated my chair around to face my staff. I simply said, "I'm sorry, but we need to end this meeting."

I remember Scott looking at me and saying, "Is everything okay?"

He knew it was not.

I didn't have to say a word.

With uninformed but heavy hearts they slowly picked up their things, stood up and walked out of my office. I remember hearing the sound of flip-flops, a deep sigh and the door clicking when it finally crawled shut. I was alone in my office, drowning in the eerie silence that rudely closed our meeting.

After five minutes or so I walked down the hall to another friend's office. He knew about the business and also knew the person we partnered with. I told him about the email, and we went back to my office so he could read through it himself. With my office still drenched in silence, I sat where Scott had been sitting during our meeting, my face in my hands, praying and trying to process all the thoughts and questions flooding my mind.

Does he have any idea of the pressures he has caused?

Was this all a part of a big scheme that I naively fell into?

What in the world is my wife going to say?

How could he do this to me? We were so close. I totally trusted him.

How could he bail out through bankruptcy . . . could he actually do that?

Should I call a lawyer first or my wife?

What is my moral obligation to these investors?

Is there anything I am now going to be held legally responsible for?

How am I going to inform the investors that all of their money is gone?

How am I going to repay all this money to these investors?

I obviously did not have answers to any of these questions at this moment. The silhouette of emotion, confusion, anger and anxiety cast a dark shadow over just about everything in my mind. I'm not sure I had any clear thoughts. I didn't totally freak out, but I clearly didn't know what to think.

When I spoke with my wife about it, of course she was equally as shocked and overwhelmed as I was. After an evening of wet eyes and intensely heavy conversation, I remember sitting by myself on my living room floor. I wasn't asking God *why* this happened. I was asking Him *what* He wanted me to do.

And now you can probably see why I thought it would be better to have Jesus physically by my side. I desperately needed to hear from God, and I needed answers quickly.

Longing for Answers

I don't know if this situation is more extreme than anything you have personally faced up to this point in your life (I certainly hope it is), but what I do know is that God taught me priceless lessons through it all. I'm sure you can relate to that.

There are always things we wouldn't necessarily choose for ourselves, and we wouldn't have strategized to work out the way it did; but through it all, we learn things we would have otherwise missed. And for this reason, after it's all said and done, we are ultimately thankful that we went through it. I say it again: I wouldn't take back what happened to me for any amount of money.

There is a lot to this situation that I will be unveiling as we move through the book. Every nuance of circumstances led me to embrace valuable lessons in following God's voice. I'll share about some confrontational and tense conversations; losing everything we had to pay back the investors; the FBI investigation; resigning from a ministry position; and many more things, including how God used this event to show me some deep-seated sin issues in my life.

Up to the point of my writing these words, I have not shared much of this situation publicly. Now I will be opening up this part of my life with the hope that the lessons I've learned will also help you in some way.

I trust they will.

As you can imagine, there were a lot of things I had no answers to. Even today, more than six years later as I write this, there are so many details I have no information on. For instance, I still don't know who initially contacted the FBI. Regardless, it was living in the midst of a slew of unanswered questions that I learned a very important life principle: <u>Operating from what we do know is far more productive than trying to find answers to everything we don't</u>.

This is an understanding to which the Holy Spirit guided me. Let me explain how I know it to be true.

I was faced with a lot of time-sensitive decisions, and the truth is that the Scriptures spoke *directly* to very few of them. I was sifting for answers, and one night while sitting at the island in my kitchen, I came across a verse that lifted the fog from the road I was now traveling. This verse, of course, didn't directly speak to how to overcome a fraud situation or how to pay back this massive sum of money or how to avoid being sued by people. But it certainly brought clarity:

> But the Helper, the Holy Spirit, whom the Father will send in my name, he will teach you all things and bring to your remembrance all that I have said to you (John 14:26).

I had read this verse countless times before and probably taught on it at least a few times as well. But as I was sitting alone in my kitchen, one word popped off the page.

"Remembrance."

I looked at that word and realized that in order to remember something, I had to have already known it. In other words, at this point I more clearly understood how the Holy Spirit was going to help me wade through these muddy waters. It didn't matter how subjective or ambiguous my circumstances were; and I didn't need answers to all the unknowns for tomorrow. I knew my Helper would guide me to what had already been told. Already been revealed. Already known.

It was at this point that I realized Jesus had already given me plenty of concrete information I was to immediately use as I sought to move forward faithfully. When I remembered a truth articulated in Scripture, I knew God was speaking to me (see John 16:13). I didn't need a physical manifestation or a mysterious cloud.

What I needed to do was trust the Holy Spirit to guide me toward the things Jesus had already taught. By doing so, I would know that God was speaking to me, and I could then move forward to do what He wanted me to do today.

Understanding this led to many of my insecurities subsiding. I grew in confidence in my ability to hear God speak. Hearing God speak to me wasn't as abstract as I had made it to be. It was actually becoming very practical.

Jesus wasn't going to be by my side physically, but He certainly didn't abandon me.

It was the foundational truths I already knew that I had to allow to drive my thoughts and actions. I had to focus on asking the Holy Spirit to remind me of what I *knew* to be true versus asking Him for what could be true or what I hoped would be true, or wanted to be true (see Ps. 19:13).

Moving Forward Faithfully

When faced with tough decisions or seemingly ambiguous ones, we pray, asking God for direction and clarity. We search the Scriptures to see if there are any direct answers to our questions. We ask others we trust for their opinion and, sometimes, we even seek the counsel of someone totally removed from the situation. By doing so, we hope to get an *objective,* or *outside,* opinion, clinging to the hope that something they say clicks with us—because nothing else seems to be. We want to do what God wants, so we continue seeking answers to all the unknowns.

Unfortunately, when we focus on all the things we don't yet know, our forward steps often halt. God can certainly bring specific answers to surface, but I would propose that spending time seeking and then waiting for God to provide these types of "answers" is not the most practical action, nor is it most helpful, for any of us.

The encouraging reality is that our process of reading, praying and seeking counsel most often reveals our desire to do what God wants. So, be encouraged. I understand how we desire God to speak to us audibly like He did when He walked on earth, or somehow give us an undeniable physical affirmation. I'm human too. But when we wait for these types of things, it's often at the expense of embracing what we already know.

This is when we know for certain that we are not doing what God wants.

Moving forward in my pursuit of reconciling this whole situation required me to take John 14:26 seriously; and when I did, I began looking into the teachings of Jesus. Knowing that I could not reduce God's will for my life to a formula that could be applied to every little circumstance, I was simply looking for principles in Scripture I knew Jesus had already taught us to live by. As I intentionally went back to the teachings of Scripture, I realized two underlying principles I already knew but now had to embrace at more sensitive levels than ever before. By seeing these things and remembering them, I knew that God was clearly speaking to me.

The question now was whether or not I was going to listen.

It's one thing to teach on truth; it's another to embrace it personally. I always seek to embrace things before I teach on them, but the truth is, I was going to have to embrace these principles in much more intimate ways than ever before.

I believe our prayers need to change from "God, show me the next steps for tomorrow," to "God, help me remember and embrace what You have already taught me so I can walk faithfully today." A desire to hear the Holy Spirit speak shouldn't lead us to beg for new revelation as much as to seek to embrace what has already been revealed.

The two principles that I find to be at the core of all Jesus' teachings are

denial of self

and

dependence on God.

These principles are foundational to everything Jesus taught and modeled.

Unfortunately, both principles not only violate our human nature, but also violently undermine our Western culture thinking.

Jesus, however, not only modeled these two life-giving principles, but He also demanded them of His followers—including you and me. They're not necessarily easy to embrace, which is why we all need our Helper; but they are simple to understand. It was when I remembered these principles and looked back at the reality of John 14:26 that I realized it was the Holy Spirit that had reminded me of these things.

In other words, God spoke to me.

I heard His voice.

It may not have been audible, but it was clear and utterly undeniable. It brought a peace within me that I could not explain, and a clarity that allowed me to move forward freely,

because

it was founded

on the truth

of Scripture.

I realized that I had two principles I needed to embrace fully if I was going to follow the Holy Spirit's leading. I found Scripture passages like Mark 8:34-35, which says, "If anyone would come after me, let him deny himself and take up his cross and follow me. For whoever would save his life will lose it, but whoever loses his life for my sake and the gospel's will save it." (Luke 9:23-24 articulates these same core principles.)

If Jesus told those who were to follow Him to deny themselves, then, practically speaking, I couldn't get caught up in protecting myself or my family in this situation. I had to think about the benefit of others, and I was to do it for the sake of Jesus and the good news of the gospel (see 1 Cor. 9:23). To do so, I had to have Him and the gospel, and not my own self-interests, in the forefront of everything I did.

When I was reminded of these truths, I knew the Holy Spirit was present in my life and working within me.

The principle of dying to ourselves isn't about pursuing poverty, nor is it saying we should feel guilty for enjoying material blessings. It is about having a focus on God and others and the furthering of the gospel. It is about seeking to put those things first, always and above any of our own personal interests or pursuits.

It's about intentionally joining in with what God is doing, not about asking God to join what we are doing. I didn't need Jesus alongside me to know I needed to embrace these principles. He had already taught them, and the Holy Spirit was reminding me of them.

The amazing thing is that when we concentrate on embracing simple truths like these, a lot of the worries of the unknown seem to fade. When they do, things become clear and we begin to move forward in confidence.

In fact, even the questions we ask begin to change. No longer was I asking for answers to unknowns. Instead, I found myself asking God to make the gospel known through me, and through my circumstances. I was asking for help to embrace what I knew He had asked me to do. Even though it may have been a bit extreme, this was an opportunity to do what was right; and because of the circumstances, it was a way I could practically embrace the simplicity of Jesus' teachings.

I learned that how circumstances *affect* us is of little importance compared to how our actions in the midst of circumstances *reflect* upon Jesus and the gospel.

Practicing Denial of Self

In regard to our investors, our contracts with them released us from all legal liability to pay back any money invested into the company, under these circumstances. But upholding section 15 and all its sub-points against people would simply be me protecting myself. It could be viewed as "good business," but it was horrible ethics. And it would have been a poor example for someone desiring to do what God wanted.

Therefore, I knew that following God's voice meant that I had to do whatever I could to get the money back to our investors.

So, taking this truth to heart, I personally committed to each investor that I would get them every penny back, even if it was the last thing I did. I didn't know how I was going to do it, but I had to depend on God to lead me. That's where the trust comes in. I knew that putting the investors before myself was right, so I trusted God to come through and take care of my family as we did so.

To be clear, I wasn't expecting God to provide a miraculous check in the mail or make things comfortable simply because I was trying to obey. I knew I was going to have to work hard; or, to use the words of Mark and Luke, "pick up my cross daily."

As painful as this was, and as much as this commitment bound me, it was probably the most liberating time in my life. I didn't embrace these principles without flaw, and I will share much of my failures in this process in the coming pages. But this is what we are called to do as Christians. Following through with the basic principles of self-denial and dependence on God isn't hyper-spiritual, nor does doing so provide a ladder for us to arrogantly climb.

Denying ourselves is a posture we take as Christians so that we further the gospel message and the name of Jesus. It's a posture that expresses our joining in with what God is doing versus asking Him to join in with what we are doing. It's a posture that actually seeks God's voice.

The apostle Paul tells us that Jesus died for all so "that those who live might no longer live for themselves but for him who for their sake died and was raised" (2 Cor. 5:15).

You see, this principle of denying self isn't just what Jesus required of those who desired to follow Him. It was also part of the reason He died. We certainly benefit greatly by His death (see Rom. 6:23; 10:9), but it is clear that His death wasn't just about our benefit.

Jesus modeled self-denial in the ultimate way, so He isn't calling us to do something He didn't do. He taught this principle with words and His example. And when we follow His example, we can be certain we are hearing God speak to us.

Paul wrote that it is an understanding of God's love for us that compels us toward a life lived for Him (see 2 Cor. 5:14). With God's love in my view, denying myself and my family some luxuries for the coming years didn't seem like such a big deal. Paying back the money to people became an opportunity to embrace the reason Jesus died.

I was a pastor, not a hedge fund manager, so paying back $945,000 was not an easy task. But by God's grace, we were eventually able to do it.

It began by selling our two homes. About a year after my wife and I were married, we bought our first home. It was a great home, but then about two years later, my grandfather passed away and I received an inheritance. It was enough to put down 20 percent on another home, so we decided to do that and rent out our first one. It was during the housing boom of the years following 2000, so it was proving to be a good investment.

When we became aware of the fraud, we had accrued just over $500,000 in equity between our two homes. As we had seen the equity rise, my wife and I often wondered how God would use these funds. We talked about all the possibilities, most of which were how it could benefit us long term.

Well, we obviously found out otherwise.

I'm not going to say that selling two homes for the purpose of giving all the money away for this reason was an easy conclusion to come to, but it was necessary, and my character was refined through it. To be totally forthright, selling the rental was an easier decision than selling the home we lived in. The sale of the rental didn't necessarily impact our daily lives. Writing out a check of more than $225,000 to other people certainly had some impact, but the practicalities of our lives were not affected. So putting this house on the market was a bit easier for us.

It was in selling the house we were living in that we felt the reality of self-denial. And it took me a few months to get to the point where I was willing to give it up. I thought it was unfair for my family to suffer for all this mess.

But I thank God for speaking to me by bringing to remembrance these basic principles of self-denial and dependence. The credibility of our word was on the line, and many of the investors were not Christian; so the testimony of our faith was on the line as well.

Asking why all this happened wasn't going to help. It *did* happen and we needed to respond with what we knew was *right*. We could have become bitter about having to pay people back, but we knew God gave us the money, and we were honestly thankful to have it so we could give it to them.

We always said the money was God's, and now we just had to embrace that truth and live out what we knew to be true. My wife and I frequently talk about our thankfulness to God for giving us the finances to get such a big head start on paying back the money.

Prior to being convicted and sentenced to a 46-month prison term, our friend paid back about $130,000. That amount, combined with the selling of our two homes, obviously gave us a huge chunk of money to pay back to investors. My wife and I were both working at the time, so we scraped together every dime possible to give back to investors. We took out a loan to pay back the majority of the rest, and then we worked hard to pay that off and continued cutting checks every month over the next few years.

Eventually, we were able to reconcile with the investors.

There are some other interesting details in regard to the timing of all this, which I will share later. But this was obviously not an easy time for us, and it certainly taxed our emotions. In fact, at one point my wife was concerned about my showing signs of depression. As I look back, I can see why she was concerned. Often, I was off into my own world, thinking about all that had taken place and all I was responsible for. And, at times, I'm sure feeling sorry for myself.

But at the core, we both knew this was the right thing to do. I didn't need God to show up in a cloud, and I didn't need Jesus to be sitting beside me to confirm what I was supposed to do. I had plenty of direction that I could stand firmly on as I moved forward.

Jesus may have left earth, but He didn't abandon me.

Neither has He abandoned you. In fact His departure from earth allows every one of us to have the Helper gently reminding us of the teachings of Jesus.

And thank God for that.

Embracing Our Helper in a Practical Way

I don't know what road you are traveling at this point in your life or how smoothly it's paved, but I do know you have a Helper that can guide you practically as you go. I want to encourage you to stand firmly on the truth of John 14:26. By doing so you will realize that hearing God's voice isn't always as subjective as you might typically think. And when you become confident in this, you begin moving forward with the help of a lens that allows you to see more clearly through whatever fog hovers.

You may not get answers to all the unknowns, but you don't *need* them to move forward faithfully or confidently. When you follow Jesus' example of putting others before yourself for the sake of the gospel, you can be certain you are in tune with the Holy Spirit.

Jesus would say the same thing if He were right beside you. Your Helper will simply remind you of that fact.

If Jesus required this principle of self-denial for His followers, and if He died *so that* we would *not* live for ourselves, then we can be certain the Holy Spirit will NOT lead us to serve and protect ourselves.

This is a truth that deeply penetrates our perceptions of Christianity. And, because our natural way of thinking goes against these foundational principles, we have to recognize and acknowledge the ways it does so. When we differentiate our fleshly thoughts from the teachings of Jesus, we will see just how much our thinking can make hearing God speak far more difficult than it needs to be.

As you will see in the next chapter, we must intentionally "incline our ear" to hear God speak, and we must also muffle other counsel. Ironically, and unfortunately, many of our sources of counsel deceive us and distort God's voice without our even recognizing it.

To help you decipher these things, I will continue sharing some of the lessons God taught me in the midst of this financial debacle. We have a couple of spiritual principles we can stand firm on thus far, but there are at least five things that keep us from hearing and following our Helper.

REFLECTION QUESTIONS

1. What do you find to be most confusing about trying to hear God speak to you?

2. When facing a decision, how has waiting for God to reveal something new hindered you from moving forward in a practical way?

3. How does the idea of first starting with what you do know change or affect your perspective on listening to God?

4. Has there been a time when God clearly showed you the next step you were supposed to take? Share that with your group. How did you know for sure that it was Him speaking?

CHAPTER 3

The Counselor Versus
External Counsels

I have a list of friends I go to for advice. Some of them live here in the Portland area, and many others live outside of Oregon. But they all know me well and have, in my opinion, God-given convictions and expertise in specific areas. Any one of them could speak into multiple issues in my life, but I tend to go to each one of them for specific things.

I go to Vanessa, Meagan or Ryan for financial decisions I'm wrestling with.

To Rick, Chris or Steve for questions about being a godly husband or father.

To Ron or Bill for church building issues. They know the Scriptures, and the ins and outs of facility usage and contracts.

For theological musings, I typically go to Todd, Tony, Matt or David.

I have many friends who pastor churches, and I call them for certain things.

There are men, women, teenagers, college students—all of them speak into areas of my life when it's appropriate.

Three days ago, I even asked my seven-year-old daughter, Karis, how she thinks I can be a better daddy, and how she thinks I can be a better husband to her mommy. She didn't say much, but she's only seven. Many more questions like these to come on future daddy-daughter dates. She'll have some insights as she gets older, and I will do my best to listen to them, for sure.

I ask a lot of people for their thoughts, and I do so on a number of different issues.

I'm assuming that you do too.

I've often asked past interns what they think I could have done better, and what sort of things they do differently now with their interns, and why that is so.

Through asking questions, I learn a lot, I glean wisdom and I believe I move forward more faithfully.

There is one friend I go to for a variety of different reasons. I go to him because of his faith convictions, and I know beyond any doubt that he has my best interests in mind. He knows me extremely well; I trust him to be honest with me, and brutally honest, if he feels it necessary. In no way is he a yes-man, and I love that about him. The last thing I want is someone to just tell me what I want to hear, so I seek his advice. After being friends for about 12 years now, I've come to know him well enough that in many situations I don't even need to ask his opinion because I already know what he would say. In other words, this friend has impacted my life, my thinking and, thus, my convictions and decisions, in a variety of ways.

Do you have a friend (or friends) like this in your life?

In the midst of decision-making processes, we go to these types of people, holding firmly to verses like Proverbs 12:15, "The way of a fool is right in his own eyes, but a wise man listens to advice," or Proverbs 11:14, "Where there is no guidance, a people falls, but in an abundance of counselors there is safety," or Proverbs 15:22, "Without counsel plans fail, but with many advisers they succeed."

Our desire to please God drives us to these people, seeking their counsel regarding our matters. We cling to and quote Bible verses like those found in Proverbs and thus feel free to schedule meetings over cups of coffee with as many people as possible, spewing out the details of our situation with hopes that God will speak to us through them.

God uses His people to speak to us.

But not always.

We still need to be careful to listen for God's voice through theirs.

We can ask so many people their opinions and end up with nothing more than a bunch of godly people who disagree with one another. It gets really confusing when each of them seems to have good reasoning for their answers. We are then put back in the frustrating position of not knowing what to do. Like the people of Israel, we become "wearied with [our] many counsels" (Isa. 47:13).

What do you do when two godly people totally disagree about your issue?

Or, how can you make sure the counsel of your friends is actually the voice of the Counselor?

As you will read later in this chapter, seeking the advice of other Christians doesn't guarantee you will hear God speak to you. I have failed to recognize this, and I see it happen all the time with others.

Incline Your Ear

A few years ago, I taught a series of sermons at Colossae Church I called, "Tuning In to God's Voice." It was a walk through Jeremiah 7:23-26, and I did this series because I believe this Scripture passage gives us some amazing insight into hearing God speak to His people. The series was largely based on lessons I learned through the fraud situation. I wanted our people to be in tune with God, hearing Him speak and being confident in their ability to do so. I taught the series to help us all toward that end.

In these verses in Jeremiah 7, we see God telling His prophet what He had already told the people of Israel. He told them to obey His voice, and if they did so, He would be their God and they would be His people.

He commanded them to "walk in all the way" He directed so that it would be well with them (v. 23).

Then we see their failure to follow God. God said to Jeremiah, "But they did not obey or incline their ear, but walked in their own counsels and the stubbornness of their evil hearts, and went backward and not forward" (v. 24).

Whoa. We need to take note of a couple things here.

First, God spoke to them, but they didn't obey. Not only did they not follow through with obedience, but they also didn't even *incline* their ear to Him. In other words, they didn't actually *try to hear* what *He* was saying.

One thing I've realized through the years is that it is really easy to read the Old Testament, see how the people of Israel constantly went against God's direction and then arrogantly think I'm above doing the same things or falling into the same traps. Somehow I think there is no way I would be that stupid. Ha. Who's to say they didn't think they were listening to God?

Who's to say they didn't talk about wanting to do what God wants, but somehow they had mistaken their own counsels for the voice of God?

Who's to say they didn't seek the counsel of friends who loved God?

Someone might say, "Well, God told them things already, and they clearly didn't follow through. He did so much for them, and they should have known that."

True.

There is no question the same would apply to us today. It would be impossible to count the things He has done in each of our lives. And He has clearly told us things to do that we fail to remember.

For instance, in the previous chapter, we looked at the principle of denying ourselves for the sake of Jesus and the gospel. It's clear that this is what God has commanded of anyone who wants to follow Him, and it is recorded in the Scriptures in a number of different ways for our reading. There shouldn't be any question on our part of what He has *already* said to us.

And yet, we easily fall into the trap of preserving and protecting ourselves while thinking we are obedient.

How many times have you followed the advice of trusted friends who counseled you to take your focus off serving others and instead serve and look out for your own best interests in a specific circumstance?

You were at peace about it because you "deserve to focus on yourself every once in a while." But you failed to see that their advice assumed you were *not* supposed to "daily" deny yourself. Their advice assumed that it's impossible to embrace the calling of Jesus on a daily basis. Their advice assumed that your life couldn't be focused solely on the gospel. By not recognizing this discrepancy, you agreed with their counsel
and thus fell into
the same
trap.
We've all done it and will continue to struggle.

The Jeremiah passage says stubbornness crept, or maybe exploded, out of their evil hearts, and we're not above it ourselves.

To be stubborn simply means we want what we want, and we won't give in to another voice. Stubbornness doesn't really want to know what other people will say. It wants others to agree with it. It's arrogant.

This is where we gain the needed insight into our own deception. For instance, Obadiah 1:3 says, "The pride of your heart has deceived you." You see, pride denies its own existence, which is why we are deceived by it so easily. Do you know many people

who openly admit to their arrogance, recognizing when it's coming out?

This passage is talking about the pride of the people of Israel,
but it certainly applies to us as well. Arrogance deceives everyone,
and perhaps mostly the one in whom it dwells. That includes you
and me.

Which leads me to two questions.

Is it possible the people of Israel were deceived so much that
they actually thought they were trying to hear God, even though
they weren't? Is it possible their deception had masked the voices
of their "own counsels" as the voice of the Counselor?

Of course it's possible, and we ought to consider the possibility that they may not have actually been as stupid as their actions
often make us think they were.

Maybe, just maybe, they were just as thickheaded as we can be.

Make no mistake, arrogance and stubbornness reside in all of
us, and we are not above their power of deception. Actually, to
deny their power in our lives is possibly the ultimate proof that
they are nestled in our hearts more deeply than we realize.

Arrogance doesn't incline its ear to anything outside its own
desires; this seems to be what caused the Israelites to go "backward" in their faith rather than forward. My hope is that we can
humbly learn from their example.

God makes a startling statement at the end of this section in
Jeremiah 7: "I have persistently sent all my servants and prophets
to them, day after day. Yet they did not listen to me or incline their
ear, but stiffened their neck. They did worse than their fathers"
(vv. 25-26).

God persistently spoke to them through people, but they
didn't hear His voice. Why? Their necks were stiff. This is a meta-
phor in the Scriptures that speaks of arrogance (see also Acts 7:51).
The harsh reality is that their arrogance led them to incline their
ear only to hear the opinions of others that agreed with their "evil

hearts." In the Scriptures, "evil" simply means to be in opposition to God's character and ways.

So, for us to say that we have sought the advice of other people doesn't necessarily mean we have heard from God. In fact, godly people can look us in the eye and say what God wants them to say, but we still might not hear it. It depends on whether or not we are inclining our ear to the Counselor or only to the counsel that will help us get what we want.

This is tricky.

I remember a friend telling me one time that he had been trying to tell me something for a long time but I just wasn't hearing it. He didn't know how else to explain it to me. I had to repent of my arrogance and ask him to tell me again.

I have watched similar things happen far too often in churches too. I have been a part of processes with people where an entire elder board has given them biblically sound counsel and yet they walk away from that advice, seeking the counsel of others. They are listening for others to affirm their thinking, and they continue asking around until they get enough people to agree with their own opinion. Once they do (and they always do), they feel spiritually justified in their thinking.

Many times, people who do this will actually feel burned by the leadership that sought to give them godly advice. Like the Israelites, God placed spiritual leaders into their lives that called them back to what God had already revealed, yet they failed to incline their ears to Him; they stuck to their own counsels instead.

A few questions:

What does it look like to incline your ear to God's voice?

How can you decipher God's voice from your own counsels?

What might your own counsels look like today?

These are vitally important questions to ask yourself, especially when keeping verses like Psalm 81:11-12 in mind: "But my people did not listen to my voice; Israel would not submit to me.

So I gave them over to their stubborn hearts, to follow their own counsels."

It might seem good at first to have your own way, but ultimately it's not worth fighting for, only to be turned over to your own counsels. Those of us who desire to do what God wants must go through the discipline of inclining our ear to the Counselor, and to Him only.

Deception is powerful. As we read about the Israelites throughout the Old Testament, we have the privilege of reading God's perspective on them. We can then arrogantly stand back and point fingers, suggesting they were total idiots. But we have to recognize the real power of deception: Those who are deceived don't realize they are deceived, which means we are all highly susceptible to deception.

The real danger is that deceived people always deceive other people. I think this snowball effect happens much more frequently today than we recognize or would like to admit.

And because of our failure to recognize it, we also move backward in our steps of faith.

Do you really,
I mean, really,
actually,
truthfully,
genuinely
want to know what
the Counselor
is going to bring to your remembrance?
I hope so. I personally want that more than anything.

If you do, too, I'd like to walk you through some counsels we often mistake as the Counselor. I can articulate these because I have failed to decipher between them myself, and I have paid a great price. I have learned that inclining my ear to the Counselor requires me to sift out my own counsels by first recognizing them.

So we will look at a few examples. Second, we must humbly and honestly address these counsels with the call of the gospel in view. That is, we have to compare these counsels to what we already know our Helper will remind us of—the teachings of Jesus. This is how we can stay in tune with what the Holy Spirit is saying to us.

That said, let's begin by recognizing two external counsels, and then in the next chapter we will look at a few internal ones. The external counsels we can easily confuse as the Counselor are the *Spiritually Unwise* and *Circumstances*.

The Counsel of the Spiritually Unwise

Today, everyone seems to think they are *spiritual*, and the number of definitions they apply to this word is vast. For our conversation, I will define *spiritual* as someone who seeks to center his or her life on following the teachings of Jesus. At Colossae Church, I define *spiritual growth* with this definition in mind. I tell our people that we can say we have grown spiritually if the amount of time between reading Scripture and embracing it is less than it used to be.

So, the counsel of the *spiritually unwise* would counsel you away from literally embracing the teachings of Jesus. The tricky part is realizing when people are counseling us in a direction that contradicts Jesus' teachings.

Even people in churches. So, we need to be careful.

Not skeptical, just cautious.

The apostle Paul spoke to this issue in his second letter to Timothy, Paul's mentee who was pastoring in the Ephesus area. Paul was writing to give Timothy instruction on how to lead the people of God, and particularly in a church context. At one point, he tells Timothy there will come a day of difficulty (see 2 Tim. 3:1) because people will be "lovers of self, lovers of money, proud, arrogant" (v. 2); and then he lists a plethora of other characteristics people will unfortunately embrace (see vv. 2-3). In verses 4 and 5 he picks up the list and says people will also be "reckless, swollen with conceit, lovers of pleasure rather than lovers of God, having the appearance of godliness, but denying its power."

Paul then tells Timothy to avoid these people. Makes sense why he would say to avoid them, right?

But here's the thing:

These

are

people

in the

Church!

Deceived by arrogance. Deceived by conceit. Proud. Lovers of self.

They were in the church in Ephesus, and they are in the church you attend. They are in the one I pastor.

These people Paul is talking about appear to be godly, but because of their focus on themselves, they will only offer counsel directed toward following the self-focused course of the world (see Eph. 2:1-3). Sure, they may be motivated by concern for you, and they may not even realize their counsel is going against the teaching of Jesus. But it is still spiritually unwise counsel, and this is why we must recognize it. Deceived people always deceive people. They can't help it. They believe something to be true that isn't; so we have to be able to sniff it out.

We all have aspects of this in our lives, which is why we desperately need our Helper to guide us toward the truth.

Spiritually unwise people will counsel away from daily dying to self and toward serving self. We know it's unwise counsel when it does not focus on the call to further the gospel, but instead focuses on selfish goals and dreams. We know it's spiritually unwise because it causes a person to take control rather than depending on God in greater ways.

This is when you need to step back with hands in the air, look into the heavens and scream, "Thank God for His grace and mercy on all of us!" We have all received such counsel. We have all followed it at times. And we have also given it.

The fantastic thing is that a true understanding of God's grace is what teaches us to avoid all unrighteousness (see Titus 2:11-14). So we must be careful to avoid counsel that doesn't push us toward literally embracing the teachings of Jesus.

It's important to distinguish the counsel of the spiritually unwise from someone counseling us to embrace the Sabbath or take a week's vacation or time away to pray for the purpose of sustainably focusing on dying to self daily and furthering the gospel, trusting God as we do so.

Unwise counsel goes beyond this. It can be seen in advice to focus on yourself, protect yourself, look out for yourself, and do so before you focus on others. The brutal truth is, they will counsel in this direction because this is how they live themselves.

I'm talking about people in churches. This is another reason why I say that just because we seek the advice of others does not mean we have heard from God. Our Helper will not say something to you through another person that violates the teachings of Jesus—you can count on that!

I ask myself two questions to help me incline my ear to the voice of the Counselor and sift out the counsel of the *spiritually unwise*:

Is this counsel pushing me to take the focus off of myself and put it onto benefiting others *and* to furthering the gospel message?

Is this counsel directing me to relinquish my pursuit of control and putting me in a place of greater dependence on God?

I ask myself these questions because they protect me from falling into the trap of listening to the people Paul is telling Timothy about in 2 Timothy 3:1-3. (You may want to look back at those characteristics to see why your answers are so critical.)

If I can answer these two questions positively, I have enough information to move forward with a confident faith, knowing that I am hearing the Counselor. This confidence leads me to be excited about engaging in the work of God, and it will lead you in the same direction.

Thank God, Jesus isn't here physically anymore, because we all need the Helper in our lives! A life focused on others and furthering the gospel doesn't come naturally. So this is one practical way that brings a whole new perspective on the Holy Spirit's omnipresence—at least for me.

The Counsel of Circumstances

Most often when we are faced with a decision, we begin by laying out the options. We do this over the course of conversations or possibly even by writing them down. As we look at and compare the options, we subsequently begin listing the pros and cons of each situation. By doing so, we hope to gain perspective that will lead us toward a God-honoring decision.

After weighing the options, we inevitably take the option that has the most points in its favor. We then move forward, feeling like we have been wise in our thinking.

Sound familiar?

But what makes us think that just because circumstances work in our favor or are easiest for us personally, we've found the option that is automatically what God wants us to do? What gives us this understanding of God's voice? Where does this theology come from?

It comes from our falling into the same self-focused traps that Paul was warning Timothy about.

By talking through the different scenarios with others, we can glean wisdom. That is, as long as we recognize the call of the gospel as we do so. We also must be intentional about remembering that we are susceptible to the deception of our own pride and can easily mistake circumstances for God's direction.

Let's look at Jonah's story for a few moments.

Yes, Jonah.

In the beginning of the book of Jonah, we see God tell Jonah to go to Nineveh: "Now the word of the LORD came to Jonah" (Jon. 1:1). So Jonah clearly knows what God has already told him to do. It's clear.

But Jonah doesn't obey what God has already said. Now watch the circumstances unfold, and let's look at them as we might process them today in our pros and cons approach.

Like us, who know what God has already told us to do on a daily basis, maybe Jonah was heading in a direction thinking to himself, *Well, I'll head in this direction and see what God does. If He doesn't want me to head in this direction, I trust He will close the door.* With this thought process, Jonah would have moved forward thinking like us . . . *an open door must mean God wants me to walk through it.*

Let's say that Jonah takes this understanding of how God leads.

In verse 3, Jonah goes down to the shipyard in Joppa and finds a ship heading to Tarshish. With circumstances like this, we might think to ourselves, *Holy cow, God provided a ship! He is sooo good! Amazing how He just works everything out so smoothly when it's right.*

The verse records that Jonah "paid the fare and went on board, to go with them to Tarshish." Based on the circumstances, we might think, *God provided the money! God is clearly in this. The doors just keep on opening . . .*

We then move forward with a peace, but it's not peace because of the Counselor, it's a peace because we are getting what we wanted. All the while we spiritualize it by telling others how the circumstances worked out so smoothly and how it is evident that we are following God.

When we head in a direction and look at circumstances that work out like this, isn't this what we think and say? When we sit with a friend who walks through all of the circumstances and see how easily they worked out in their favor, aren't we amazed by how God just worked everything out perfectly?

Quick question as a checkpoint: What if Jesus had pursued doing God's will with our view of circumstances to determine His actions? Jesus clearly did not model our understanding of circumstances as the means to determine God's will. If He had, He would not have gone to the cross!

Unfortunately, even though the circumstances were seamless for Jonah, the end of Jonah 1:3 says he was heading "away from the presence of the LORD."

The counsel of circumstances can easily drown out the voice of the Counselor. Circumstances that work out in our favor and make things easier for us can be a means of God's leading, but they are clearly not always His leading. And, with the teachings of Jesus in view, and our pursuit to embrace them fully, we might even consider being more cautious when circumstances do work out perfectly in our best interests.

We must always check our circumstances with what God has already revealed for us to do. At the very minimum that means we depend on God as we deny ourselves daily and join in with what He is doing.

You won't see that view on a late-night self-help commercial, but you will see it in Scripture.

And the Scriptures are what we cling to for understanding as the Helper calls to our remembrance the words within them. Here are two questions I ask myself to make sure the counsel of circumstances are not drawing me away from the voice of the Counselor:

Does this put me in a position of dependence on God?

Throughout the Scriptures, God calls His people to depend solely on Him, so I know the Holy Spirit will always direct me toward that as well.

*Will this push me to a deeper commitment to what I already know
Jesus taught?*

I can articulate these things only because of my own failure to
always incline my ear to the Counselor and weed out these external counsels. All of this really began to come into perspective when
I was dealing with the fraud situation. I not only saw my failures,
but I also saw the true depth of arrogance and self-focus within
my heart. My pride was deceiving me and causing me to react in
emotion and overlook my own sin.

Envy was driving many of my decisions.

Greed was counseling me toward certain things.

I'll open up that part of my life in the next chapter because
seeing the failures of someone else might help you avoid falling
into the same trap.

REFLECTION QUESTIONS

1. As you learned about the people of Israel in this chapter and
   their struggle to listen to God, what similarities do you see in
   yourself?

2. Up to this point in your life, how has the unfolding of circumstances affected your understanding of God's will? Has this
   chapter changed your perspective in any way? If so, how?

3. Has this chapter changed who you will seek advice from or
   what you will seek advice for? If so, how? If not, has it affirmed
   any previous convictions you've held?

CHAPTER 4

The Counselor Versus
Internal Counsels

It was a Saturday night, the first of four services our church had every weekend. I was sitting off to the far left front of the stage, feeling somber and emotional. My wife and a dear friend, who drove three hours to support me, were sitting on either side of me. I was having a hard time grasping what I was about to do.

This was the first of four times I was going to stand in front of the thousand people in the room and tell them that a day earlier, on Friday morning, I had resigned from my position at the church. These were people I loved, and they loved me, and yet I was about to publicly drop a bomb in their lap. I didn't know everyone on a personal level, but they knew of me, and I at least knew most of their faces.

The hardest part about this announcement was that I couldn't be completely forthright as to the reasons why I resigned. Because the FBI was investigating our case, we were placed under subpoena by the District Attorney to not give any details to anyone, in any way, about the situation. And I certainly couldn't mention the fact that the FBI was investigating. I'll share more about that investigation soon, but basically the only information we could give at this point was that I "started a business outside of our church" and circumstances were at a point where I had "to step out to take care of responsibilities pertaining to that." So, that's basically all that our pastor said. Ambiguous for sure, but we spoke all the truth we could.

He then brought me up to say a few words. I had asked to share because I was noticing a few things in myself and I felt like I needed to be honest with everyone about those things. The people in our church deserved to know. I didn't have a ton of time to go into great detail, but I did want to let people know that I was seeing some things I needed to work on. I realized this confessional on top of the already ambiguous disclosure could confuse people, but I felt like they deserved to know as much as we could tell them. So I let them know I was seeing some sin issues in my life that needed to be addressed.

Arrogance.

Greed.

I could at least be completely forthright about those things.

To help them understand my perspective, I gave an illustration. I told them to imagine they were looking up at a beautiful mountainside on the Italian Riviera. There were trees with pastel Italian homes peppered throughout the foliage. Imagine Tuscan vineyards below and a train traveling from left to right on the mountain base. Steam rose from its smokestack. To the right there is a beautiful tunnel the train will soon enter. From a distance it looks like a black and white Ansel Adams photo. Shadows just right. Looks even more perfect the further you stand from it.

But then I asked people to imagine walking up to that tunnel the train was approaching. It looks beautiful with everything else around it, but you walk into the tunnel and it's a different texture. Dark. Damp. Trash on either side of the tracks. Graffiti on the interior walls. Things you never saw prior to entering it.

I told them this is what I was seeing in my own heart; and even though it has some beautiful parts to it, there was some trash that needed to be picked up. Some graffiti to be scrubbed away. I told them I felt like my stepping away was time in which God was allowing me to do such things. And I felt obligated to be honest about the pride, greed and envy I was now seeing within myself.

It's part of repentance. And it's beautiful.

Sure, the whole announcement put me in some uncomfortable situations. One person was telling people she thought I had cheated on my wife with a business client. A few others asked me if I was running some sort of multilevel business, using my position at the church to recruit people. One time I was sitting with an elder from the church in a coffee shop when a guy cornered me, angrily trying to get me to tell him what *really* happened. He didn't believe it had something to do with a business situation. I tried to kindly remind him that I wasn't at liberty to say anything about the details, but everything was going well and I was working hard at taking care of our responsibilities.

He was very rude, pointing out that "church leaders are never honest," so he wasn't surprised that I was "a coward, hiding from the truth."

It is moments like this when it is hard to remain humble. Hard to keep my mouth shut. It's in moments like this when emotions can easily counsel me away from humility and wisdom but instead toward defensiveness. Thankfully, I had self-control in this moment and ended the conversation as graciously as I could. The elder who was with me knew of the inner workings of this situation and helped me exit the conversation as graciously as possible.

Tough circumstances, regardless of how they are perceived, make it hard to control emotions. Thankfully, through my failures, I learned a lot of valuable lessons about the power of emotion, how to filter its counsel, and the balances necessary to incline my ear to the Counselor. I'd like to share some of that with you, even though I'm still far from perfect in this area.

The Counsel of Emotion

I remember sitting in a church service one day, a few months after resigning, and a guy I had mentored was leaving for the mission field. The elders and pastors were asked to go up on stage and pray for all that was to come in his life. I was sitting in the aisle seat, heartbroken that I was not a part of this moment in his life. My eyes filled with tears of gratitude for all God had done in this guy's life . . . and there were also some tears of envy. I wanted to be one of those praying for this guy, and I felt like I deserved to be able to do so.

The real kicker came when I had to physically move my legs into the aisle so that another pastor could squeeze by and go up and pray for this young man. This pastor just so happened to be the one who stepped in to cover all my responsibilities. He was now leading the ministry I started from scratch six years earlier.

It was a vivid picture that will forever be embedded in my mind. God gave it to me. He taught me much through it, not only to reassure me that my identity was not in a ministry position, but also to reveal how much emotion and envy were counseling me. It was in times like these that I had to watch the counsel of my emotions and intentionally tune in to the Counselor.

I had to focus on what I knew to be true about God. He loved me and was going to continue to teach me by using whatever circumstances He placed me in. These "trials" had rhyme and reasoning to them (see 1 Pet. 1:6-7). It wasn't about me personally, nor was it about my feelings. This was all about Him.

Fighting the tension between emotion and truth can be difficult. I'm an emotional being, and I think this is a fantastic part of who we are as people. Emotions allow us to feel. To relate. To identify. To engage.

Emotions are potentially our strongest influencers. The power they possess is great, and yet when unidentified and untamed, they not only affect our feelings but also how we think and, therefore, what we do and say. They counsel us. We don't typically think about it this way, but our emotions counsel and push us in directions. Sometimes they are godly directions; sometimes they are not.

We need to recognize their power and appropriately direct them. This is easier for some than others, but the psalmist Asaph articulates a fantastic journey through his emotions in Psalm 77, which I think applies to all of us.

Asaph was a Levite man who ministered at the Ark of the Covenant. He was a recorder by vocation, but a musician at heart. As a human being, he got emotional; and in this psalm, he let us into that part of him. I think you will be able to relate to his feelings a bit here.

In Psalm 77:1-4, we see Asaph troubled to the point of having no words to describe his feelings. He is desperately and consistently seeking the comfort of God, but he gets to a point where he loses hope. He doesn't feel like God is there for him.

Have you ever cried out to God and felt like He wasn't there for you? Ever wondered if He's listening? You don't feel like He is, and so you wonder . . . ?

Verses 5-9 articulate a journey of his emotions festering. He wonders if God has withdrawn favor from him, ceased to love him, is failing to follow through with what He has promised or has simply forgotten him. Asaph even wonders if he did something wrong that God is angry about. These are normal human thoughts and questions.

Emotions are extremely powerful counselors, and they always affect our thinking.

God is surely there and loves him, will always follow through with what He promises and definitely still has compassion on Asaph. But Asaph has allowed his feelings to define his relationship with God.

That is dangerous.

✳ His emotions are distorting these truths and telling him otherwise. As great as emotions are, they can also get us thinking in a direction away from the truth of Scripture. Our emotions can cause us to embrace the lowly, feed the hungry and help the widow. But in other times, like Asaph's words show, they direct our mind away from the road of truth the Counselor would tell us to travel.

Emotions can cause us to question God versus depend on Him.

Emotions can cause us to lose self-control instead of exhibiting the fruit of the Spirit.

To say things we don't actually mean.

To make decisions we later regret.

To lash out defensively.

To focus on our feelings rather than on truths we already know intellectually.

They can even get us to the point where we try to spiritualize our sinful reaction.

They can get us to envy others.

They can get us to lose hope.

And they ultimately rewrite history to justify their actions.

At the root of all these directions is a focus on self. Emotions can even lead us to a point of self-pity, feeling like we deserve more or better than our current circumstances. ✳

I had some moments like this when I was dealing with the circumstances I was placed in with the fraud case.

I wondered why *I* had to go through this.

Was all this really necessary to teach me these lessons?

✳ A grave danger inherent to the counsel of emotions is that they cause us to focus on and preserve ourselves. This is why our emotions need to be grounded in truth, focused on the things Jesus has taught and God has done. In Psalm 77:10-20, we see Asaph take an intentional step back and put his emotions in check. He begins to remember "the deeds of the LORD" (v. 11). He takes his focus off his *feelings* and places it on what he knows to be true about God. He looks back, remembering the things God has accomplished and what He is capable of and what He has promised.

It was these things that Asaph could stand firm on and what turned his depressed feelings into hope. Tuning in to our emotion will lead to feelings of hopelessness. But remembering what God has done and is capable of leads to hope. We can always expect feelings of hopelessness when we're constantly focused on ourselves. On the other hand, focusing on what we know to be true about God leads us to hope. And this is also what leads to the inclining of our ears to the Counselor.

If you've lost hope in your marriage, then focus on what you know God is capable of doing. Remind yourself of all He has accomplished despite the brokenness in other marriages. I have seen God turn a marriage around where the wife left her husband and children to live with her own blood brother. Yes, you read that right. And yes, your worst assumption from that statement is probably the correct one. If God can reconcile a situation like that, He can reconcile yours as well.

If you get emotional about finances, rely on what you know Jesus taught about God's provision if you are seeking and engaging in the things of His kingdom first (see Matt. 6:33).

If you struggle with anxiety, trust in the truth Jesus has taught us: it accomplishes nothing (see Matt. 6:27).

I know, it's easier to say that than to follow through. I have failed too. But we can all pursue the voice of the Counselor and seek to muffle our own counsels from within as we fight that battle.

Emotional Breakdown

I remember sitting in an office with three elders. We were discussing my plans to pay back the investors. Out of concern for me, they were simply asking questions. They were taking time out of their day to help me process through this. And like any friends or leaders would, at times they were challenging my thinking. They loved me enough to try to help me recognize how my emotions had gotten my thoughts off base. I remember getting defensive as if they were attacking me. I don't think they knew I was feeling like this at the time, but they saw me get emotional. I didn't blow up, but I did break down.

Tears streamed down my face as I began pouring out all my insecurities, questions and frustrations. I just let it all go.

And, to be totally forthright, my emotions caused rank thoughts to cross my mind. In the midst of this breakdown, I was thinking about the people outside of that office who were telling me that nobody would question my integrity if I chose not to try to pay people back.

I thought about how much easier it would be for me and my family to just leave and take another position at a church out of state.

I thought, *Why am I continuing to attend this church and subjecting my family to all this pressure and ridicule?*

I thought, *I wasn't the one who did all this, so why should I be the one to pay the price of paying everyone back?*

This was precisely the beginning of my realizing how much I had allowed the counsel of *emotion* to take over my thinking. As powerful as my emotions were, I still could have controlled them.

If I was expressing the fruit of the Spirit, I would have exercised self-control and reeled back my emotions and held them up to what I already knew to be true. What I knew for sure. What I knew about the call to follow Jesus.

In other words, that's a nice way of saying I didn't obey God's voice but was instead "following my own counsels." I had put the focus on me and my circumstances, rather than on those who had lost their investment. I was focused on preserving myself.

It may not feel good to check our emotions with what we know to be true, but it is critical to do if we are to incline our ear to the voice of the Counselor. Let me walk you through a couple of questions I ask myself now to help me see whether or not I'm inclining my ear to the Counselor:

Do my feelings and decisions follow what I know God is capable of?

This is important because emotion might be leading me toward trying to control what I am fearful God will *not* do. When we fall into this trap, we can know for sure we are listening to the counsel of emotions versus the Counselor. I knew God was capable of giving us the finances to do what was right. I knew it could require me to work very hard; but for the sake of the gospel message being furthered, and for the name of Jesus, God was certainly capable of coming through. I needed to deny myself, do what was right and depend on Him as I did so. This is when I grew in confidence that I was, in fact, inclining my ear to hear the Counselor.

Is this decision leading me toward a gospel-centered versus a self-centered mindset?

This is where I really dive into the gospel call to deny myself and depend upon God daily. If I am focused more on my feelings or experiencing feelings of envy, I quickly take a step back and intentionally process how I can avoid falling into those traps.

If I can answer these two questions positively, I then move forward with confidence that I have heard the Counselor speak to me.

The Counsel of Greed

I had some great motivations for going into business. My wife and I really believed this was a means by which we could live our dream of working in ministry but not taking money from the church. We often talked about people and ministries we hoped to be able to help financially. My wife has an MBA, and I have an entrepreneur-ial mindset, so we thought this was a way we could steward *all* of who we were . . . for God.

All these were great motivations. They sounded spiritual, and these are what I focused on as I moved into starting a business. What I failed to do was intentionally recognize the greed that had army crawled up to the perfect sniper position. I've found most people fail to do this. We focus on our godly motivations and share those with others to the point where we gain their approval and then move forward as if we are in tune with God.

Yes, maybe.

But, maybe not.

In order to truly gain wise counsel, we must also recognize and disclose where our impure motivations are to godly, gospel-centered people.

On stage, as I shared with our congregation about my resigna-tion, I gave them another illustration. Putting my palms together and aligning my fingertips I held up my hands with one set of knuckles facing the crowd and one set facing me. I told them the knuckles facing them represented the impurities of my heart and those facing me represented the pure parts (by aligning your hands in this way you can really only see one of the hands . . . in fact, you can only see one side of one of the hands).

I held the "pure" knuckles close to my nose and told people this has been me over the past year. With my arms extended I then flipped the "impure" knuckles around so that I could see them. I told them this season of my life was about making sure I was noticing this side of my hands. Again, not able to give them de-tails regarding the business situation, I was hoping they would at least see there was good in my departure.

God's will is for all of us to be like His Son, Jesus (see Eph. 4:13), and this was a means by which He was bringing me toward that end. This was good. Expensive but good.

Throughout this process of investigating my own heart, I realized that greed abounded far more than I would like to admit. It was quietly squatting behind the walls of every pure motivation. As I looked back, I started to recognize the nights I had a calculator out and was trying to figure out how much money we could make and the different scenarios that could lead to making more. I started to think about how many early mornings I had spent trying to figure out different angles to talk to potential investors at different Rotary gatherings or with a group of businessmen I would occasionally run into at the golf course.

Some people might suggest this is what you do in business. I understand that, and I'm not saying that making money is wrong. I'm not even saying that trying to make *more* money is wrong. People don't usually go into business to lose money, so I get it. But what I can say is that after asking God to reveal my true heart motivations, I began to see that much of my pursuit of making money was sinful.

Again, I certainly had some pure motivations. But that's not the point here. We always concentrate on those things. The point is that I didn't recognize the power behind the counsel of greed and how much it was pushing me toward the pursuit of more money.

Greed causes us to fantasize about having more than what God has supplied. More possessions, more money, more . . . even when we say we're content.

Greed is manipulatively self-seeking, deceptively allowing us to think we are focusing on others while we are actually focusing on ourselves. The reality is that once we want something, we will do what we can to get it. This, at best, clouds our thinking.

Greed is rooted in arrogance, which is deceitful. And herein lies its danger. Because we are not intentional about recognizing where greed has burrowed itself into our hearts, we easily give in to its counsel. Greed counsels us to get more but can and often does deceive us into thinking it's for the sake of others. We buy a boat and say it's for youth events. We buy a bigger house to be more hospitable. The boat and house are likely used for events, but there is greed in there too. The question is whether or not we recognize it.

I've found that very few people actually believe that greed exists within them. But, to muffle the counsel of greed in your life is a starting point for inclining your ear to the Counselor.

Sins like being prideful or lustful or struggling with anger tend to be easy for people to admit to. Greed and envy, however, are another story. Because these are so deceitful, I ask myself four questions in order to muffle the counsel of greed out of my life:

What are my sinful desires in this decision?

We can never rid ourselves of all sin and impurity, but we can at least recognize where they are. Spiritual maturity does not mean ridding ourselves of all sin. That's the job of the Holy Spirit (see Phil. 1:6). Spiritual maturity recognizes where sin is and then places guardrails up to protect from falling into those desires.

What do I have to gain in this?

I ask myself this question to make sure I am at least aware of the self-focused motivations that might be influencing my thinking. My goal is then to try to limit how these affect my decisions. This is a practical way I seek to deny myself and literally follow the words of Jesus. By doing so I am inclining my ear to the Counselor.

Who am I going to tell about these sinful desires and selfish pursuits so that they can help me keep them in check?

This is important for me so that I don't deceive myself into believing my thinking is biblical when it's not.

Do my spiritual authorities affirm this decision?

This is important because I can ask enough of the wrong people to make sure my emotions and desires are appeased and affirmed and met. They may even empathize with my feelings of envy. Seeking this kind of approval from others might give the façade of spirituality, but the goal isn't to get what I want. The goal is to do what God wants and to join in what He is doing. To walk on the path He leads me down. To listen to Him, and to Him only.

Final Musing

I share all of this with you because noticing these things within yourself is vital for the process of inclining your ear to the Counselor. Jesus says that when the Helper comes, "he will convict the world concerning sin and righteousness and judgment" (John 16:8). This gives us confidence that when we are convicted of sin, we are, in fact, hearing His voice. Jesus came to wipe away our sins once and for all (see Heb. 10:12-17), so recognizing and repenting of them is a practical way in which we glorify Christ (see John 16:14-15).

The hard part of all this, and I know this to be true because I've had to wrestle through it myself, is that recognizing your sin often leads you to feelings of shame and guilt rather than to Holy Spirit-led repentance. After resigning, I dealt with intense feelings of shame. How could I put my wife and family in this position? How could I have let so many people down? How could I have allowed my emotions and greed and envy to overtake my thoughts at such deep levels?

After 10 months, and after working through so many of these heart issues, I was rehired on staff at Cornerstone. It was a tremendous feeling to be back. It was great for me and I honestly believe it was great for our church—few people see a pastor leave a church and then return. But, for me, it was taking the 10 months to sift through the sin in my heart that led me to a much healthier place. I was able to move past the feelings of shame and to a healthy point of recognition. When we move toward feelings of shame and guilt, we are *not* hearing the Counselor. You can be certain of that.

Discerning the difference between godly conviction and feelings of shame can be tricky, which is why we now move on to chapter 5. If there is an area that we must be certain we are inclining our ears to God and God only, this area of discernment is certainly one that requires attention. If there is any issue stifling the people of God from freely and confidently engaging in what God is accomplishing today, in my opinion, it's shame. As we will see, this is an unfortunate pattern throughout history.

That's just a way of saying we're not alone. You'll see what I mean.

REFLECTION QUESTIONS

1. Do you tend to be more logical or emotional when it comes to the way you approach life? What are some of the positive things about your natural bent? What are some of the dangers?

2. Have you ever thought about the power emotions have over your thinking? If so, how does this chapter compare to your previous thoughts? If not, how has this chapter opened your eyes to that reality?

3. How do you think these internal counsels are affecting your prayer life right now?

4. What can you do to continue to muffle their voices and incline your ear to hear God, and Him only?

CHAPTER 5

Comforted in Our Imperfection

I am a Christian because I know I'm not perfect.

This reality is at the core of the Christian belief. There is nothing we can do to make ourselves perfect or right in God's eyes. No amount of accomplishments. No amount of hard work. No amount of good deeds (see Eph. 2:8).

It is only,
and I mean *only*,
through what God has given us
in Christ
that we can be made right
or justified
in God's eyes.

Consider taking a moment to set this book down and read Romans 3:20-28.

To be fully aware of our imperfection and inability to be perfect on our own is to recognize the beauty of the gospel. This is why we cling to the hope of Christ. And yet, for some reason, Christians are ashamed to admit to and be honest about these areas of their lives.

Am I the only one who finds this odd?

We embrace Christ because we know that we are consistently imperfect; and yet we have a hard time admitting the ways we are imperfect. Doesn't that seem to undermine everything we claim to believe?

Now, I might not be the smartest guy in the world, but I'm not a complete idiot. I get that sometimes we don't even recognize our wrongdoings, possibly because of the deception of our own arrogance. Or sometimes, if we do recognize our sin, our arrogance leads us to be horribly concerned about what others may think, to the point that we don't want to say anything. The idea of someone holding these things against us in a judgmental fashion can be quite threatening to the image our arrogance wants to uphold.

Everyone abhors this kind of mask on others but feels the need to put it on themselves. Interesting.

This is nothing less than hypocrisy driven by the arrogance within us.

It is a twisting of truth for the purpose of self-protection.

We go through all sorts of intellectual gymnastics to avoid admitting our sins to other people. But our arrogance often leads us to a place of confusion that is much less likely to be talked about. So I want to bring that up.

I'm talking about how we confuse faithfulness with perfection.

Let me explain this further because there is a massive difference between the two, but it is very easy to confuse them. I've found that when people think about being *faithful*, most tend to think of being *perfect*. When they think about having a day of faithfulness, they think of a day without sin.

This is bad theology and misses the truth of Jesus' teachings and the voice of our Helper, turning the Christian faith into a guilt- and shame-driven religion. This also leads us to arrogantly judging people and withholding our confessions from them. But for our topic here it's important to realize that in the midst of all this mess, we fail to hear God speaking. The Holy Spirit does not lead us to believe we need to be perfect. He will instead comfort us in our imperfection.

You Are Not Alone

Many people constantly deal with guilt because of their imperfections. This could be guilt for something they've recently done or something they did in the distant past. Regardless, they are somehow constantly reminded of their wrongdoing. They are stifled by feelings of shame and regret, and they can't seem to get past the guilt. The phrase "I can't seem to forgive myself" summarizes too much of their thinking.

Because guilt and shame abound, some people try to make up for it by working harder or trying to do more good deeds, thinking this will somehow right their wrongs. The guilt and shame in others cause them to run away from God, from the things of God and even from the people of God. They shamefully shrink back and move backward in their faith, feeling alone in their imperfection. They think they are the only ones struggling with *their* particular issue.

Can you relate to any of this? If so, know that you are normal. These feelings are, unfortunately, part of being human.

But it is vitally important to understand that none of these feelings of shame and guilt are the voice of the Holy Spirit in your life.

He will not speak guilt and shame into your life. Conviction, yes, but not shame.

The Holy Spirit convicts you and leads you toward God.

Shame will guilt you into disengaging from God because you feel like there are things you need to get straight before you go to Him.

There is no comfort in shame. No hope. No gospel. No Jesus. We've already discussed how the Holy Spirit will never guide us to serve ourselves; but it's also important to understand that He is the Comforter.[1] And when it comes to sin and shame and guilt, we desperately need Him to comfort or help us with the truth of Scripture.

I have done some horrible things in my life—things that used to haunt me and did so for quite some time. I've had a child aborted. I've caused pain to others intentionally. I've stolen. Lied. Manipulated. Cheated. And, as I've already shared, I've been at the root of people losing a lot of money—some of which was a portion of their retirement.

All of these things were tough for me to move past. But the abortion was probably the hardest. When I became a Christian, this was the one thing in my past that really stood out to me. It kept nagging at me and was something I could not seem to get over. In theory, I understood that God forgave me; but for all practical purposes, I couldn't accept it. I guess you could say I couldn't forgive myself.

Wherever I went I would see people with their children. In stores, coffee shops and parks, I would immediately picture how old my child would have been. Feelings of shame and guilt would crash against the rocky shore of my mind, capsizing my theology in a manner that caused me to run from God. Not outwardly, of course. I was too proud for that. I would run inwardly. I couldn't go to God with confidence, because I knew my sin.

My shame caused me to wrongly view God as someone to run from because of my sin. Instead of openly and intimately going to God, my shame was guiding me progressively farther away from Him.

I know I'm not alone in this.

I may not know you, but I know that a normal part of being human is to struggle with this tension. That is to say, I realize you know these feelings too.

The first book in the Bible shows us that guilt resulting from sin was a human problem from the very beginning. After both Adam and Eve had eaten of the fruit God had told them not to eat, the intimacy between them was broken. They hid their bodies from one another in shame (see Gen. 3:7). But most unfortunate is when they heard God's voice, and their shame drove them to hide from Him (see v. 8). They were fearful and thus viewed God as someone to run from because they had sinned.

This is what the guilt of sin does. And it does it to all of us, at least to some degree. This is why we must be very careful to incline our ear to the Comforter.

Our arrogance leads us to believe that we should be above sin and thus bombards our mind with shame and guilt when we fail.

In contrast, the Comforter leads us to a deeper understanding of His grace and mercy so that we recognize our inability to be perfect and thus cling to the truth of the gospel. But He doesn't lead us in this direction by feelings of shame and guilt as the motivators.

An understanding of God's grace leads us toward avoiding all unrighteousness (see Titus 2:11-14).

When you recognize your sin, you can be confident that God is speaking to you. When that recognition leads you to feelings of shame and guilt, you can be confident that He is not.

Instead, when God speaks, He leads you to Himself in true repentance that will culminate in accepting grace and mercy and forgiveness and then embracing the freedom and joy that come from them.

Faithfulness Versus Perfection

When we confuse faithfulness with perfection, it is a clear result of our pride and arrogance. We tend to think we're too good to fall into temptation. We think of ourselves as people who should be *above* that. And it shows when we don't match up to our own perceptions and thus have feelings of shame.

Ha! Come on now. We all know ourselves better than that. We can't be perfect; that's why we are Christian—that's why we follow the One who is perfect. If we're honest with ourselves, we know how "off" we are. We just need to be reminded of this reality. And yet, in the midst of our imperfections, we also desire to be faithful. This is a paradox that few people seem to be able to grasp or balance. How can we be faithful and imperfect at the same time?

Glad you asked.

I would like to show you an example of this balance in and through the life of King David. David is held up as the model king of Israel. And God used him in very powerful ways to carry out His purposes.

At a time when the people of Israel had gone through a dozen leaders who all ultimately failed to be faithful (as seen throughout the book of Judges), Israel was left longing for a faithful leader (see 1 Sam. 8). In 1 Samuel 9, we see how God appointed Saul as the king of Israel; and then in chapter 10, Saul is presented to the people as their king. Unfortunately, Saul was not a good king; by chapter 15, we see the prophet Samuel telling Saul that God has rejected him as king (see 1 Sam. 15:22-23).

A side note related to our conversation thus far: Saul actually thought he had been obeying "the voice of the LORD." Take a moment to look at that in 1 Samuel 15:20-21. Saul had convinced himself that he was doing what God wanted him to do, and he was arrogantly blaming the people of Israel.

Back to David. Following this encounter, even though Saul eventually recognizes how he has not upheld the commandment of the Lord (see 1 Sam. 15:24-25), Samuel lets Saul know that God has "torn the kingdom of Israel" from him and has "given it to a neighbor . . . who is better" than him (v. 28).

Harsh words. Well, this *neighbor* was David. Saul's reign over Israel doesn't actually end until he dies, but God is not "with him." David is standing on the sidelines with "the Spirit of the LORD" upon him (1 Sam. 16:13). We also see that God's Spirit departed from Saul (see v. 14).

Interesting transition.

We then see David defeat Goliath. This is more than a cute Sunday School story. There was a lot at stake for the people of Israel. Had David lost this battle, the people of Israel would have been the slaves of the Philistines (see 1 Sam. 17:9). The future of the nation rested on this battle. God uses David to defeat Goliath, showing His power (see vv. 46-47); and through all of this, God gives David an unbelievable platform, one that causes much jealousy to come upon Saul. With his jealousy counseling him, Saul tries to kill David at least twice.

Eventually, Saul dies, and in 2 Samuel 2 we read that David was anointed as king of Judah. Israel was initially passed down to Saul's son, Ish-bosheth, but in 2 Samuel 5 we see David defeat him in a battle, making David king of all Israel. David *faithfully* served as king for a total of 33 years. As we read about David in the Scriptures, he is clearly the model king, anointed by God.

God even said David was a man after His own heart (see Acts 13:22).

But David was far from perfect.

He lied to the priest at Nob, resulting in his death (see 1 Sam. 21-22).

David sought revenge against Nabal, trying to kill him simply because his ego was hurt. Fortunately, Abigail stopped him, confronted him and convinced him to turn away from his vengeance (see 1 Sam. 25).

He used his position as king to have sex with Bathsheba, a married woman, and got her pregnant (see 2 Sam. 11). He then tried to cover his tracks. Everyone knew her husband was out fighting the war for David. Therefore, it would have been obvious that she committed adultery. She would have been a social outcast, punished by the religious leaders and could have even been killed. David, knowing this, sought to salvage the situation and cover up his sin.

He sent his men out to get the husband, Uriah, off the battlefield. They bring him back to David's house. David meets with him, asking how things are going on the battlefield. He then tells Uriah to go down to his own house (see 2 Sam. 11:8). David's plan was to have Uriah go home so that he could "be with" his wife, assuming her pregnancy would then make sense to everyone. People would see Uriah in town and know that he was home. Bathsheba would then be saved from the coming ridicule, and David's sin would be covered.

Uriah doesn't go home, but instead sleeps on David's doorstep (see v. 9). The next morning, David finds this out and asks him why he didn't go home. Uriah responds by saying, "My lord Joab and the servants of my lord are camping in the open field. Shall I then go to my house, to eat and to drink and to lie with my wife? As you live, and as your soul lives, I will not do this thing" (v. 11).

Uriah is a man of principle. He does not think it's fair for all the men to be out there suffering and him to be in his comfortable home with his wife. Why should he have all that when they are still out sacrificing their lives fighting?

David, on the other hand, is being counseled by his own selfishness. He wants to cover his sin. He is focused on protecting himself.

So David tries a different strategy. The next evening, David wines and dines Uriah to the point of getting him drunk. In this drunken state, David is confident Uriah will lose sight of his fellow soldiers and stumble his way to his own home.

But Plan B doesn't work either (see vv. 12-13). This is a major problem, because David desperately needed Uriah to go down to his house so people would see him and then assume Bathsheba's baby was Uriah's.

With the failure of Plan B, David then does the unthinkable. He sends a letter to Joab, his military leader, with orders to put Uriah on the front lines where he would surely be killed. David actually tells Joab to put him in the front and "then draw back from him, that he may be struck down, and die" (v. 15). Joab does as the king commands, and Uriah dies (see v. 17).

Clearly, David commits murder and is guilty of Uriah's blood. To top it off, he takes Bathsheba as his wife, assuming that everyone would then view him as the "good king" who reached out to the poor widowed woman. They would then understand why she was pregnant, since the marriage had to be consummated.

With all this in mind, we could say that David is a lying, egotistical, adulterous murderer who got lazy and allowed his sex drive to overtake his focus. Some might even argue that he raped Bathsheba.

Sheesh.

This is the faithful king? The man after God's heart?

It is, most certainly, an interesting dichotomy—one that we must be able to wrap our minds around. The moment you confuse faithfulness with perfection is the moment you sign up for a miserable life drowned out by shame and guilt.

You will miss God's voice.

You will miss the good news of the gospel.

You will turn the Christian faith into a horrible religion that nobody wants to be a part of.

Faithful Imperfection

About 10 chapters later, in the book of 2 Samuel, we read a song written by David. It will blow your mind. Take a few moments, open your Bible, and read just a portion of this song in 2 Samuel 22:21-25.

Seriously, set this book down and pick up a Bible to read those few verses.

Are you shocked or surprised at David's words? Do you wonder how he could say such things after all he had done?

I propose that he can say, "The LORD dealt with me according to my righteousness; according to the cleanness of my hands he rewarded me" (v. 21) because faithfulness and perfection are not the same things. You see, after this whole Bathsheba and Uriah incident, David's friend Nathan confronted him (see 2 Sam. 12), and then David did something we all need to do more of.

He repented.

He admitted and fully recognized his sin and then ran to God with it. In so doing, he was being faithful. We see his confessional in Psalm 51.

He recognizes that God is the only one who can make him right (see Ps. 51:1-2). He acknowledges that he has wronged God (see vv. 3-4) and that his very nature is bent toward moving away from God's ways (see v. 5). He also sees the reality that God wants him to be honest with the truth within himself (see v. 6).

True repentance always entails honesty, but many people fail to incorporate it in their practice of repentance—which clearly doesn't make sense. We need to be truthful about how we have wronged others and God. Then we can be certain we are hearing God speak. Too often, Christians are so ashamed of their sin that they can't even think, much less utter their sins in a prayer. They ask God to forgive them for "that thing," or they go to God saying, "God, You know what I've done . . ."

We need the full truth in our inner being, practicing vulnerability and intimacy with God in our confession. Our confession must be honest with the harsh reality of our sin. If it is not, it is not true repentance.

"Forgive me; I was selfish and killed an unborn child."

"Forgive me; my greed has led to the loss of many other people's money."

"Forgive me of my selfishness that makes my child feel like she is a nuisance."

Do some of your statements of repentance sound like these?

"Forgive me for giving attention to that man's pursuit of me and neglecting to follow through with my word of remaining faithful to my husband in all good and bad times."

"Forgive me for giving in to the counsel of greed and lying on my taxes."

"Forgive me for secretly looking at pornography and lying to my wife about it."

"Forgive me for envying my sister. I constantly compare my husband to hers, and this is causing me to belittle and demean my own husband."

These phrases of confession should be wrapped up with the words of David, "Against you, you only, have I sinned and done what is evil in your sight" (v. 4).

This is what it means to have truth in our inner being.

This is what it means to be honest with our imperfection.

This is what we do when God speaks to us.

Like David, we can be faithful, and we can be certain that freedom is around the corner where the Comforter will soon meet us with His grace, mercy and forgiveness.

David sprinted toward God for cleansing of his "bloodguiltiness" (v. 14), fully recognizing that God is the only one who could restore a clean heart within him or restore him to the joy of his salvation (see vv. 10-12).

After being restored by God, David experienced the Comforter, the Spirit of truth, the Helper. He knew that he could then move forward, engaging in all God was doing (see v. 13) and he would praise God (see v. 15). David realized there was no amount of good things he could do or offer to God to make himself right (see v. 16), but it was only a humble and broken spirit that God would accept (see v. 17).

In all of this, David was faithful.

Imperfect but faithful people recognize their sin and run to God with it in truthful confession, resulting in repentance that restores intimacy with God. Faithful people realize that God's grace isn't an excuse to sin, but rather it is a teaching tool to avoid it (see Titus 2:11-14). When they are reminded of this truth, they recognize that the Holy Spirit has spoken to them.

Imperfect but faithful people experience the Comforter when they understand that only God can make them right.

Imperfect but faithful people experience the Comforter when they accept His grace and mercy after repentance and engage with God, the work of God and the people of God. But we sometimes need to be reminded of this reality.

Imperfect but faithful people know that God has spoken to them when they go through this process, because they are fully aware there is nothing within them to cause them to think or act in such a manner.

If you desire to do God's will, it's because the Holy Spirit, your Helper and Comforter, has given you that desire. The fact that you desire to please God should bring comfort (see Ps. 40:8). I have seen too many people beat themselves up because they are not perfect; and many, because of their imperfection, even end up questioning their salvation because of their lack of ability to be perfect.

So I would encourage you to make sure you keep this in check and filter out the counsel of shame and guilt. When, and the key word is "when," you fail to perfectly follow through with your desire to please God (see Rom. 3:23), you can be faithful to genuinely repent, experience the grace of your Comforter and continue to join in all that God is accomplishing.

Walking Reminders

When my wife and I were expecting our first daughter, we were thinking of names, as every expectant parent does. We went through all the lists. At one point, I asked my wife if we could name her Karis. I liked the name, but my desire for it stemmed much deeper than just liking the name. It was a vocabulary word I learned for a Greek course in seminary (that's essentially grad school for pastors). The word *karis*, or formerly transliterated as *charis*, means "grace." In certain contexts, the root word can also be translated as "joy," but it's usually translated as "grace."

Although I had worked through true repentance and had honestly received God's grace for the child I aborted earlier in my life, there were natural consequences of the sin that I was still battling. I couldn't just forget about it. And at times I struggled to embrace the reality of God's grace in my life, particularly over that issue. Much of my struggle was rooted in my own pride. Some of it was rooted in a godly sorrow. Some was rooted in regret and shame. To battle these things, I had to focus, and still do, on the truth of the grace and forgiveness of our God (see Heb. 10:11-15).

This is one reason I asked my wife if we could name our daughter Karis. In the first place, I believe it is only by God's grace that I was able to have another child. I certainly didn't deserve to, but God graciously allowed it. And I thought it would be an expression of my realization of this fact. But it was also a wonderful walking, breathing reminder to me of that truth.

And Karis is that—a true blessing.

All of my girls are named after truths I need to be constantly reminded of.

We named our second daughter Hope. She is another walking reminder of the truth we are certain of in Christ, and the fact that all of my hope should be placed in Him (see 1 Pet. 1:13).

Our youngest daughter is Sayla. Her name is the English way of saying *selah*, as seen in the book of Psalms. *Selah* is the Hebrew word for "to listen." Not only is listening a powerful characteristic to possess, but she will be a walking reminder to make sure I'm listening to God and taking His truths seriously.

We, of course, pray for our daughters to embrace the truth found in each of their names. People sometimes joke about these being "pastors' kids' names," but I obviously hold them as very dear to my heart. The mere thought of those little girls brings tears to my eyes as I write this.

So much joy.

So much peace.

Before we wrap up this chapter, I encourage you to be confident that you are hearing God speak to you when your recognition of sin leads you toward the process of true repentance and the grace of your Comforter. Maybe you can find some physical reminders in your own life that will help you keep shame and guilt in their proper place.

This is absolutely critical to your Christian life. When you have feelings of shame and guilt, you will withdraw. You will disengage from God the same way people have from the very beginning of time. Remember Adam and Eve's attempt to hide from God? You will disengage from the things of God and the work He is doing, and the work He wants to do through you. You will also disengage from the people of God—the people He has given to you as family, as a means for building you up toward the maturity of Jesus (see Eph. 4:11-15).

God will not lead you away from such things.

REFLECTION QUESTIONS

1. After reading this chapter, how would you express the difference between shame and conviction?

2. How have shame and guilt haunted you? How have they driven you farther from God, rather than closer?

3. How does differentiating between faithfulness and perfection affect your view of God? How do you think it will impact your prayer life?

4. How does this chapter's articulation of what repentance is compare to your common practice of repenting?

Note
1. The Greek word for "helper" can also be translated as "comforter." It is translated this way in numerous translations, such as the *King James Version, New International Version, American Standard Version* and *Young's Literal Translation.*

CHAPTER **6**

Comforted into
a Lifestyle of Faith

Living by faith can seem scary and risky, which is why many people choose not to walk in it. If that describes you, I pray the Holy Spirit helps you overcome those fears.

Let me begin by telling you about a man whose daughter was on her deathbed.

The once joy-filled 12-year-old girl was now lying lifeless on the bed she used to jump on when her parents weren't watching. Everyone around had given up and accepted the fact that this little girl's struggle to live would soon end. Her father was not willing to give in to that thought—I can't imagine any parent easily giving in to that idea. Instead, he sought out Jesus and asked Him to heal his little girl. Begged Him. Earnestly implored Him.

After seeking Jesus, in his time of need, this father clearly heard Jesus say He would heal his little girl. Incomparable peace filled his soul.

And then she died.

What is a parent to do in a situation like this? In one moment this guy hears Jesus say his daughter is going to be fine—He will heal her. The next moment, this father hears that she has died.

x

In moments like these, people get frustrated. I've heard people say that God told them something was going to happen, but it didn't. People have told me they knew for certain God said He would take care of something in a specific way, and then He doesn't.

The words "God said . . ." or "God told me . . ." are a sort of trump card many people pull out. Often, this card is used to somehow feel spiritual about following one's own decisions and actions. Ultimately, I have found that many people who have made such statements without the results they expected rarely come to a point of humility of considering the possibility that they didn't hear God as clearly as they thought; they confused their own desires and expectations with God's voice. So they hold firm to what they think they heard and end up questioning God. Usually, they struggle with anger and bitterness toward Him too.

The biblical story of the father and his daughter near death is a little bit different in one way. This man, Jairus, was physically with Jesus, so he literally heard the voice of Jesus (see Mark 5:21-43). In a last-ditch effort, Jairus went out into the villages, found Jesus and personally asked Him to heal his dying daughter. He believes that Jesus is capable of healing his daughter, so he asked Him to do so.

This was a bigger step for Jairus than you might realize. Jairus was the leader of the Jewish synagogue in the area. The other leaders had continually ridiculed Jesus for the uproar He was causing. Jesus had undermined their authority, and what is potentially even more threatening, He had brought the political ruling power's dreaded attention to this religious world. The Romans had left the Jews alone, for the most part, to operate as they wished since they weren't causing any problems at all. But now, with all the healings and miracles Jesus was doing, there were village uproars that everyone was hearing and talking about. This had the Jewish leaders concerned that the Romans would set up standards that imposed on their religious practices. It was a major concern for

Jewish leaders and was partially the reason they tried to undermine Jesus' ministry.

It had to take some serious guts for Jairus, a well-known leader
in this religious world, to publicly go up to Jesus and bow down at
His feet. The other religious leaders could have abandoned Jairus
right there. But he pocketed his pride and risked his religious pres-
tige because he believed Jesus was capable of healing his daughter.
And, just like those of us who take steps of faith based on what we
know Jesus is capable of, Jairus didn't know for sure if Jesus would
actually do it. But his fear of what may or may not happen didn't
stop him from stepping out.

That's a very important point in this story.

Jesus agreed to heal Jairus's daughter. But on their walk back
to the house, Jairus's friends inform him that his daughter is dead.
This is probably when the emotionally charged intellectual gymnastics began for him. A thousand thoughts must have raced
through Jairus's mind.

He was probably thinking he should have never left his daughter's side. He could have been there when his daughter died. The
thought of living with this regret would have been paralyzing.

On the other hand, he may have been thinking he tried everything possible but now it was just too late. Losing a child has to be
one of the worst feelings, if not the worst feeling, a human being
can experience. But maybe he was thinking he at least tried everything within his power.

Maybe there were some doubts racing through his mind too.
He could have been thinking that maybe Jesus wasn't really as
powerful as He thought He was . . . or He wouldn't have said He
would do something that wasn't going to happen.

Regardless of our speculations, this is when Jesus, in a way
that only He could do, made a statement that cut straight to the
heart. Jesus looked into Jairus's eyes and said, "Do not fear, only
believe" (Mark 5:36).

Those are powerful words for a variety of reasons.

First, Jesus clearly set fear in opposition to belief. This gives us insight into the inner workings of not only Jairus, but of all human beings. People are driven by fear rather than belief much more than they would like to admit. The truth is, we can respond out of fear *or* we can respond out of belief. It's an either-or issue; so we must be able to distinguish the two.

To tell Jairus not to have any fear in a circumstance like this must have been like telling him to grab an inner tube and paddle across the Atlantic Ocean. Of course he had fear! He didn't want to lose his daughter.

Second, Jesus' statement was powerful because following the counsel of fear leads us to a different place than the counsel of faith and belief. Jesus clearly knew this, and that is likely why He took this teachable moment with Jairus.

It is in the midst of emotionally charged circumstances that things get very blurry for any person. Jairus was going to either begin operating in fear of what Jesus might not be able to do, or he was going to walk in faith, believing that Jesus would still do what He said He would do.

Distinguishing between fear and faith deserves much more attention. So let's continue by simplifying the idea of living in faith.

Simplifying Faith as a Lifestyle

Faith is often less scary, less adventurous, and can even be far less "risky" than most people tend to believe it to be. The concept of living by faith is often limited to nothing less than having a "jump first and fear later" attitude where one is left wishfully thinking God has to come behind them and bless their direction simply because they took a personal risk. Some people think of faith as the idea that God somehow tells you to do something nobody else has ever done or no one has done in this particular way; or that giving every last dime of savings is the only way to *really* live by faith.

I believe that these extreme and limited ideas of living by faith, for lack of better terms, are causing fear to arise within Christians in a paralyzing way. Faith might entail aspects of these ideas, but doing these things could also be nothing less than sinful steps of presumption where God is held to whatever expectations you hold appropriate (see Ps. 19:13).

I would suggest that living a life of faith can be, and often is, much more mundane than any of these ideas. You don't *need* to have some out-of-the-box, audacious dream in order to live by faith. You don't *have* to do something nobody else has ever done to step out in faith. You don't *need* to change your geography to feel like you are living in faith.

Living by faith is simply moving forward in obedience, trusting that God always does what He says He will do. Fear, on the other hand, would halt us from moving forward in obedience, because we are consumed with anxiety over what God *may not* do. Faith leads us to a point of dependence on God; fear leads us to depend on ourselves and to seek control.

This is a very big difference.

To make it as practical as I can, let's go back to two basic truths we know Christians are called to do: *deny self* and *depend on God*.

For this conversation, we can then say that faith is a consistent focus on denying ourselves for the sake of others and to further the gospel, and depending on God to take care of us as we do so (see Mark 6:7-12). We do what Jesus has told us to do and then trust Him to do what He said He would do. When we live like this, we live a *lifestyle* of faith.

I've found that more often than not, living by faith is not as much about what you give up as much as it's about what you focus on. It may help to think of walking in faith as focusing your life on being obedient to what you know and then depending upon God to take care of your needs.

When this is your focus, you can be certain the Helper is helping you, because there is nothing within you that would drive you to embrace these truths. And when you take these steps of faith, you will also be comforted. People who take huge steps of faith often feel moments of nervousness, but they mostly feel comfort and peace because they know that what they are doing is right, even when other people are freaked out by their step of faith.

I remember stepping out to plant Colossae Church. A lot of people were asking me if I was scared. I wasn't, but they were. There were certainly moments when I wondered what in the world I was doing; but when God calls you to do something, there is also overwhelming comfort and peace as you walk it out. This is evidence of the Comforter's presence in your steps of faith.

I recently had lunch with a couple from our church. They are adopting a child from Africa who is HIV-positive. They are not scared at all and don't have any concerns about their other son. But some people on the sidelines are freaked out by this idea. But not them. They are convinced that God has called Christians to care for orphans and widows in some fashion, and they are personally embracing that calling by adopting this boy and depending on God to care for their needs. Taking this step of faith and focusing on what they know is right has allowed them to feel the Comforter at work in their life.

They have chosen to operate in belief rather than fear.

There's another couple in our church that had to sell their house but, because of the economic downturn, they ended up owing more than they could sell it for. They could have walked away from it like many others have done, but they had made a commitment to the bank. They wanted their yes to mean yes (see Jas. 5:12), so they sold it for whatever they could get and have now developed a payment plan to pay the remaining $30,000 of the original amount they said they would pay. It was hard for them to even get the bank to respond to them so that they could make payments, but they pursued it until they put a plan in place. They didn't necessarily know how they could pay it off, but they stepped out in faith, doing what they knew was right and depending on God to meet their needs. In doing so, they have experienced the Comforter in tremendous ways.

I sought to do the same thing when paying back the money invested in our company. I knew it was the right thing to do, so we stepped out in faith, trusting God to care for our family as we did so. By living this out, we experienced the comforting personal presence of the Holy Spirit like never before.

Many people don't feel the Holy Spirit's comfort like this because they don't take the steps of faith to do what they know is right. Instead, they operate out of fear of what may or may not come to pass. They live with all the fears of the unknowns in mind and then seek to protect and preserve themselves. That's the natural thing to do, so I understand.

But Jesus didn't want Jairus to fear; He wanted him to believe.

Fear of What May Not Be

Jesus addresses this issue of fear versus faith in Matthew 6:25-34. Jesus is teaching against cultivating anxiety about tomorrow. More pointedly, He is addressing the concept of worrying about whether or not our most basic needs will be met. He is telling people that instead of operating in fear of what may not be, "Seek first the kingdom of God and his righteousness, and all these things will be added to you" (Matt. 6:33).

Paraphrased, Jesus is saying, "Focus on the right things and depend on God to care for you." He isn't promising prosperity here. He is promising provision for the necessities of life. Jesus is teaching that anxiety and fear rob us of faith and dependence on God, and the comfort of the Holy Spirit.

Your specific geographical location and your lack of genius ideas are of little importance. Being obedient to God and then depending on Him to take care of you personally equals living by faith. You may not be able to see how your needs will be met tomorrow, but that should not be of concern (see 2 Cor. 5:7). When you focus your mind on denying yourself for the sake of the gospel, doing what's right and then depending on God, no other signs are necessary to test if it's of God (see Mark 8:11-13).

The harsh reality is that the counsel of fear and anxiety will drown out the voice of the Comforter in your life. Fear of what might not be is anything but peaceful. It is threatening and detrimental to a lifestyle of faith. The burden of fear is heavy, not light (see Matt. 11:30).

Jairus had to choose between operating in fear—never again being able to feel the warm smile of his daughter against his cheek—or operating in faith—believing Jesus would come through with His word.

Jesus makes it clear to Jairus which path he should choose.

Belief.

Not fear.

However, again, far too many people tend to live in fear, anxious of what might *not* come to pass, instead of operating out of belief and moving forward in faith. We worry about what God might *not* do or take care of, even though He has already told us He would provide for our necessities (see Matt. 6:25-34).

We even worry about *how* God will do it; and because we can't figure that out, we often don't move forward faithfully.

Fear of what might not happen becomes our focus and serves as nothing less than a thief to faith.

To step out in faith required Jairus to trust Jesus at face value, to fight his fears of what might not be and to walk patiently up to his daughter's limp body. The story, of course, is yet another example of how Jesus always follows through with what He says He will do. He brings Jairus's daughter back to life. I'm sure that Jairus had some doubts about what was going to take place as they walked toward his house. This is normal. But he kept walking with Jesus despite the fears and doubts. He trusted Jesus.

And this is vital to walking in faith.

A certain amount of questions or even doubts is a normal human reaction, but don't let them stop you from doing what you already know you ought to.

As I think about that, a scenario comes to mind from my own life. I remember the first time the FBI knocked on my door to investigate the fraud situation. At the time, I didn't even know they were involved, so their arrival was surprising to say the least. To this day, I still don't know who initially notified them, but I certainly remember the feelings of fear that enveloped my body as I opened the door to find two men in suits, briefcases in hand and badges raised. I can still remember the feeling of heat filling my cheeks as the blood thrashed through my veins.

I let them in, and for the next few hours I sat at the island in my kitchen answering all their questions. I was dealing with all sorts of fears as I explained the ins and outs of what happened. I remember multiple times being fearful of how my answers might negatively affect me. This fear was actually causing me to consider twisting the truth a little. There were a few points that I thought a little twist might better protect me and my family. All this internal struggle was going on even though I knew deep down we hadn't done anything wrong.

It's crazy how much and how easily our fears will drive our decision-making processes to a point where the Holy Spirit will never lead us.

The reality was that I didn't know what any of this was going to mean for me. What I did know was that I was becoming concerned about our association with the lost funds and the possibility of some type of legal consequences for me.

Because of my fear of the unknowns, I was tempted to lie.

I know it doesn't make sense. I didn't even know the impact of the truth, so I'm not sure why I thought lying would help.

Well, I do know why. It was the fear of the unknown drawing me away from what I knew was right. It was a scheme. In the heat of the moment my emotions were proving to be extremely powerful counselors.

By God's gracious help, I was able to decipher these counsels versus the Counselor's voice. He comforted me toward embracing what I knew to be true and only articulated the brutal truth. Because of my commitment to follow Christ, I knew that I could not lie (see Col. 3:9). So, I did what I knew was right and depended on God to do what He willed with it. If I had done something wrong, then I trusted that He would bring justice in that.

It was unnerving, for sure, but there is always comfort in doing what we have been called to do. That's part of what living by faith is all about.

Part of this investigation included looking at every aspect of our finances, from our business account to our personal accounts, and being totally opened for examination and scrutiny. This ended up being a part of what vindicated us from any legal responsibility; but having the FBI comb through everything is pretty uncomfortable. As they were going through all the records on our computer, I sat in another room, filled with fear.

The bottom line of my sharing this is that I want you to know I needed to embrace what I knew Scripture had told me to do. And whatever that meant, I trusted God to take care of the basic necessities for my family. I had to trust that He would do that for us even if it meant my going to jail for something I didn't even know I did. The fear of the unknown could not make me take a detour from what I did know. I had to tell the truth.

Embracing faith as a lifestyle is truly that simple. You focus on and do what you already know you are supposed to do and

then trust God with the consequences, whether those are positive or negative.

Faith as a Spiritual Discipline

It's in situations like this that walking in faith requires a *tremendous* amount of discipline. When we think of spiritual disciplines,
we usually think of Bible study, prayer, fasting, tithing, and so on.
We want to be faithful, and so most of us have been taught that we
should embrace all of these habits and behaviors.

There is much to be said about a life of discipline. We know
that God has given us the ability to exercise self-control and discipline (see 2 Tim. 1:7). We know that organizing our life creates sta-
bility in our faith (see Col. 2:5), and that we must discipline
ourselves if we are to be godly (see 1 Tim. 4:7-10). In other words,
not only is discipline good, but it is also necessary.

I find it interesting, however, that I have never seen "living by
faith" in any list of spiritual disciplines! All of my experience shows
me that faith takes a tremendous amount of discipline on my part.
There are a lot of things that will counsel me away from doing
what God has called me to do and then fully depending on Him.
I have to be very intentional to sift through outside counsels; I
have to fight arrogance that draws me away from God in shame;
and I have to put up guardrails in my life to make sure I am not
moving backward in fear.

This is why I decided not to ask anyone to join our church plant
and didn't build a team. I needed to put myself in a position where
I knew God was bringing those He wanted to join. It's also why I
didn't fund-raise or ask our sending church for ongoing support.
I didn't want to question whether our church was growing because
I fund-raised or because God was doing it.

I certainly don't think it's wrong to build a team, nor do I
think it's wrong to fund-raise. But it would have been for me. I was

called to take this step of faith, and I needed to set up guardrails to make sure I was continuing to do so. In all of this, I have to be disciplined and pray for the Holy Spirit's help to truly depend on Him. Your guardrails might be different, but whatever they are, you will need to be disciplined to put them in place.

All other "disciplines" can be great, but let's be honest about this. Most of us hold up the traditional spiritual disciplines as the markers of what faithfulness looks like. We believe that if we can follow through with all these things—do our "quiet time" every day, serve in the church, pray, fast—we will then be faithful. And when we don't uphold these standards, we feel guilty.

The problem isn't in doing these things; the problem is in setting them up as *the* markers of faithfulness. This was the core problem of the Pharisees. They believed they had to do certain things continuously and not do other things in order to be faithful. If they deviated from these "laws," they weren't being faithful.

Isn't this exactly what we do?

When someone asks you how you are doing in your faith, don't you immediately think about how much you've been reading your Bible or how much you've been praying or whether or not you've been attending church?

In other words, you believe that if you don't uphold all these habits and behaviors others have set up for you, you're struggling in your faith. There is some truth in this, and embracing these habits is wonderful, but we must understand that Jesus came because we cannot consistently uphold the law. Ultimately, they don't even keep us from doing the wrong things (see Col. 2:20-23). We know this, and yet most of us still fall into the trap of thinking we have to "do" these things in order to be faithful.

Living by faith and depending on God isn't even among the lists of spiritual disciplines.

I personally find that fascinating, especially since it's really all that Jesus calls us to do. Jesus has not called you to embrace the spiritual disciplines, as we know them. He has called you to a life of faith, of which those disciplines are often a by-product.

If anything, living by faith and depending on God ought to be at the top of any spiritual disciplines list. And I might even go as far as saying they should be the only ones on the list! I say that because when I am embracing faith as I have described it, and depending on God

I read my Bible

I pray fervently

I fast

I serve

I give

I meditate on Scripture.

In other words, when I am living by faith, all these disciplines follow, and I actually want to embrace them. The spiritual disciplines are a by-product of a lifestyle of faith, not creators of it. Why do I say all this? It's because we have to realize that the Comforter will not lead you toward embracing manmade markers of faithfulness; the Comforter will lead you through and into a lifestyle of faith in which you are more and more disciplined in every area of your life.

You may need to read that sentence again.

If you want to feel the Comforter in your life, avoid laws and embrace a lifestyle of faith where you focus on being obedient and then on depending on God. When you do, you can be certain the Holy Spirit is at work in your life, and you can be certain God has spoken to you. You can also be certain that you will be helped in areas of discipline.

Thank God, Jesus isn't physically here, because every one of us needs the uncontainable Holy Spirit to help, guide and comfort us into a lifestyle of faith.

Augustine (AD 354–430) said, "Faith is to believe what we do not see; and the reward of this faith is to see what we believe." Today you may not be able to see the inner workings of tomorrow, but your faith will one day allow you to see the only One that matters.

God will honor your steps of faith because He calls you to live by faith. He will honor your obedience and dependence by meeting your needs. Your faith in Jesus doesn't guarantee anything but eternal joy and celebration; but even if a lifestyle of faith means we downsize our homes and give up our entire savings . . . it is more than worth it. As you take steps of authentic faith in the mundane aspects of your life, I pray you feel the Comforter come alongside you and give you a peace that transcends the understanding of anyone on the sidelines . . . and even your own.

REFLECTION QUESTIONS

1. What is most scary to you about taking steps of faith?

2. How does this chapter compare to your own thoughts on taking steps of faith?

3. How have your fears of what may or may not happen affected your steps of obedience?

4. How have those fears counseled you away from the Holy Spirit's direction?

5. Have you ever thought of faith as a "spiritual discipline"? What do you think about it now?

CHAPTER 7

Counseled in the Midst of the World

When I first became a Christian, I threw away all of my secular CDs. In my mind, this was a marker of my relationship with God. I was saying that I was going to leave my old life behind and move forward with Him as a new creation (see 2 Cor. 5:17). It was a symbolic act that is still meaningful to me to this day, but also one that leaves me a bit unsettled now.

When I first became a Christian, I broke up with my girlfriend. We had been dating for over three years. In my mind, this was taking a step away from engaging in relationships that were not godly, and a commitment to pursuing purity in my life. I am thankful for my desire to pursue purity, but I am not totally settled on how I went about it.

When I first became a Christian, I stopped hanging out with the friends in whom I had invested years of relational energy. In my mind, this was a needed step away from a lifestyle of self-indulgence. It was yet another step toward purity for me, but also one that I look back on now with some ambivalence.

You may look at those steps I took early on and say, "Amen!"

If so, I kind of agree. I say "kind of" because although these may have been appropriate steps for someone in my position and background, the truth is, I had wrong thinking that was driving much of those decisions. I guess there could be nothing less expected . . . I was an infant in my faith.

I remember talking on the phone with the girl I was dating, arguing about belief in Jesus. The conversation that sticks out in my mind made her feel inferior as a human being because she didn't believe what I did. My separating from her may have helped me in some areas, but it certainly didn't help her understanding of who Jesus is. In fact, I'm fairly confident it distorted her understanding of Him.

I remember telling my group of friends that I wanted to head in a different direction in life, which inherently meant I was leaving them behind. The way I approached that, in both action and word, made them feel like they didn't matter to me at all. Because of that, my stepping away from them painted a picture of a Christian that wasn't exactly the life Christ modeled for us.

My motivations were mixed, and my thinking was both dead-on yet totally off. Part of me was simply trying to please God. But I was off in that I actually believed that in order to be faithful as a Christian I had to disassociate with "those types" of people. I couldn't hang out with my friends who were continuing to party and use drugs if I wanted to pursue Christlikeness. I couldn't be around my girlfriend, because she might defile me and cause me to sin again.

As if *she* was the problem.

I was told that when it comes to sin issues, I had to "run in the opposite direction." There is much truth in that statement, and it is certainly necessary in many different circumstances. But if we are not very careful to make some distinctions, this thinking can also cause us to lose sight of why we are Christians in the first place.

There are times when we need to step away from certain things for a time because we just can't seem to avoid falling into sin. But we must make sure that our decisions for a time don't become patterns of separation as a lifestyle. Unfortunately, this pattern can easily be embraced because of deeper beliefs that often counsel our steps away from things and people "in the world."

And even though we think of these ways as being godly, they are not.

To find balance, what we need to be is gospel-centered. In our pursuit of holiness, we cannot lose the larger picture of all that God is doing. We must make sure that we are paying attention to the teachings and calling of Jesus, to following what He modeled in His everyday life. I would suggest that when we are balanced this way, we begin to define "wisdom" differently than separating from everything "unclean."

Separating is not wise thinking, and it certainly is not Christ-like living. It's actually arrogant, and in direct opposition to the message of the gospel.

I encourage you to take about three minutes to set this book down right now and read Galatians 2:11-14 to see that point being made by the apostle Paul.

The reality is that the Holy Spirit leads us to be witnesses to those outside our religious circles (see Acts 1:8). Separating from those outside our religious world is precisely the mentality Jesus spoke harshly against. He actually opposed this lifestyle pattern by the way He lived and taught. Therefore, we know the Holy Spirit won't lead us in a different direction. Let me explain this concept a bit more, because it is crucial to following God's voice in your life.

Deceived by the Pharisee Within

The Pharisees were a group of people that lost the balance of engaging with people outside their religious circles. This imbalance was actually rooted in arrogance. They followed their own religious routines rather than the example of Christ. Unfortunately, we often struggle, like I did, with falling into the same patterns.

The Pharisees were self-appointed watchmen of the Jewish faith. They understood a lot of things correctly, but they also lost the heart behind much of what they did. For instance, they placed a high value on memorizing Scripture, which is obviously a great value and practice. Just because they knew the Scriptures did not mean they were applying them appropriately.

Take, for example, Jesus' conversation with the Pharisees recorded in Matthew 22:37-39. This passage is known as The Great Commandment.

The rabbis (whom the Pharisees followed) had divided the Mosaic Law into 613 separate laws. They said there were 248 positive laws and 365 negative laws. They had a whole system figured out. Since they had all these different divisions and rankings of things they ought to be doing, they assumed that Jesus would have a system as well. So, when they went to Jesus and asked Him what was "the greatest of the commandments," essentially they were asking Him, "What is the most important thing we should be *doing*?"

To answer their question, Jesus quoted from a passage of Scripture found in Deuteronomy 6:4-9, known as the *shema* (the Hebrew word for "hear"). The faithful Jewish people recited this passage twice a day, every day. The Pharisees copied this text on small pieces of parchment, put them in small cases and wore them on their foreheads and left arms (around the bicep area) during times of prayer. It may sound like they held this passage dear to their hearts, but their knowledge wasn't playing out in appropriate ways. In fact, Jesus actually rebuked the Pharisees for wearing these (see Matt. 23:5) because they were only wearing them to look holy to other people.

Faithful Jews would also put this passage in *mezuzahs* (small boxes) and place them on the doorposts of their home, with the exception of the kitchen and bathrooms, because those were deemed unclean.

Needless to say, the Pharisees were very familiar with the passage Jesus quoted.

Jesus' response to them shows us something interesting. Jesus answered their question by quoting a section of this passage called the Shema: "You shall love the Lord your God with all your heart and with all your soul and with all your mind" (Matt. 22:37). In a sense, He was saying, "You recite the passage every day, you bind it on your arms and foreheads to make yourself look good on the outside—and yet you don't know what you're supposed to be doing?"

Jesus cut through all the behaviors and habits and got to the heart of the issue. They were going through all the motions but missed the point. They memorized Scripture but weren't loving God. They knew the Scripture passages but weren't applying them. They lost the heart of God and began to create their own ways of thinking and doing things.

For example, their misunderstanding led them into the trap of thinking they had to separate from everything unclean or secular to remain faithful to God. They wouldn't associate with certain people; they wouldn't eat certain foods and they developed a ton of rituals for cleansing themselves from the "impurities" of the world—both from things and from certain types of people.

Fundamentally, they believed that in order to remain faithful to God they had to separate from the secular things of the world. They fully believed that certain external things would defile them. For example, in Mark 7:1-23, we read that they had developed washing rituals to keep themselves from being defiled from these things. In this particular situation, the Pharisees noticed that Jesus wasn't following these rituals, so they asked Him why He wasn't doing what they were doing.

Jesus made a few critical points as He addressed their question. For instance, in Mark 7:6-7, He said they were hypocritical for two main reasons: (1) they honored God with their external actions, but their hearts were not in it, and (2) they were teaching their habits of behavior of separation as if they were ordained by God.

I know that might be a lot of information, but stay with me for a second.

These statements made by Jesus violated the Pharisees for a couple reasons. First, they actually thought it was their external actions of cleansing and separating themselves from various things in the world, and adhering to specific habits and behaviors, that brought them closer to God. However, Jesus defined this mentality as actually being far from God.

Did you catch that? It's important.

He later made it clear that all their rules and standards ultimately disregarded and made void God's commands (see Mark 7:13). Their thinking led them to set up standards as being equal to God's standards. They then deemed anyone who didn't uphold *their* standards as unfaithful, which is why they asked Jesus why He wasn't doing these things.

If He was truly the Messiah, wouldn't He have the same separatist mentality as they did?

Jesus' point in this whole passage is that it wasn't the external things that defiled them, and there was nothing they could separate themselves from that would keep them pure. Instead they were defiled themselves (see Mark 7:20-23). Their arrogance led them to think of themselves as higher than others. Their arrogance led them to think they had to separate from the world in order to pursue holiness. Their arrogance led them to the mentality of completely disengaging from the world and creating their own bubble of rituals and relationships to keep themselves from being defiled.

This idea in Christian circles is called living in a "holy bubble."

I call them "unholy bubbles."

Unfortunately, we see the mentality of the Pharisees creeping into churches across the world today. And people who have this separatist mentality actually think it's holy thinking.

This is not holy thinking.

It's arrogant thinking.

And if I'm honest, this was the unhealthy arrogance that drove many of my decisions when I first became a Christian. I was told that these things were bad and that I needed to make sure I had an entirely new community of people around me. This meant that I had to leave all preexisting relationships behind. The bottom line is that I believed "those things" and certain people in the world would somehow defile me. Some Christians even go so far as to think that everything in the world is our enemy.

We have to recognize the fact that this is exactly what the Pharisees thought and was one of the main reasons Jesus was so harsh with them in conversations.

(I should have put exclamation points at the end of that sentence.)

Jesus made it clear to the Pharisees that there was nothing they could possibly separate themselves from to keep from being defiled. Jesus instead made it clear that the problem lay within their hearts, which debunked their arrogant practices of separating from everything in the world (see Mark 7:20-23).

This is a critical distinction to make, because following Jesus, and therefore hearing God's voice in your life, requires a recognition of this mentality within yourself. In order to engage in the work of God, you have to engage with things in the world, not separate from it. When we look at the teachings and life of Jesus, this is abundantly clear. To separate from the things in the world in these ways is to follow the thinking of the Pharisees, not Jesus.

The problem is that we haven't yet seemed to figure out what it means to be "in the world but not of the world."

The Prayer of Jesus

To follow Jesus doesn't mean you have to engage with *everything* in the world, but it doesn't mean you separate from everything either.

You need balance, which is why Jesus prayed for you.

At the end of Jesus' life, and before He went to Jerusalem to be crucified, He prayed to God for Himself and for His followers (that includes us). This high priestly prayer is recorded in John 17. Jesus made it clear that He had accomplished the work God gave Him to do (see v. 4); He had taught His followers the words of God (see v. 8); and He began to pray for those who chose to follow Him (see v. 9).

He was very clear with His prayer.

He again said that He had given them God's word (see v. 14), and then made it clear that He was not asking God to take them *out of the world* but instead to protect them as they *continue living in* the world (see v. 15).

Catch that?

He prayed this because their identity was not of the world (see v. 16). But make no mistake, they were expected to live in it. Jesus made this point abundantly clear again in verse 18, when He said, "As you *sent me into* the world, so I have *sent them into* the world" (emphasis added).

Purposefully sent into the world. "Engagement" is a good word. Because Jesus holds His sending as the definition of our sending, we know our sending requires engagement with the people outside our religious circles.

In verse 20, Jesus said that He is praying for anyone who is to follow Him from that day forward, which includes you and me!

Have you ever realized that Jesus actually prayed for you when He prayed the prayer recorded in John 17, assuming that you would follow Him and engage in the world?

Have you ever stopped and really thought about how He came into the world to model a life for us to follow and now has sent us out *into* the world to continue His mission?

With passages like this, what do you think leads Christians to believe that we have to separate from the things in the world in order to truly follow Him?

The answer to that question will be different for each of us. We all have different fears and theological misunderstandings that would lead us away from engaging in the world.

But I can tell you who, for sure, is *not* leading you to that thinking.

The Holy Spirit.

He will not tell you to separate and to seclude yourself in an unholy bubble. You can be confident of this fact because Jesus sent us into the world and modeled what that looks like for us.

This is tricky. If we're not careful, we can mistake the Spirit's leading toward Christian community as an end, rather than a means to an end. We want to learn more so we get involved in a study. We're told we should serve in the church so we take another night a week to do that. Our kids are involved in youth programs. Our spouse has a different study to attend. In all of this, we talk about our fleshly struggles with sin issues and our need for true accountability. These can be wonderful things!

But before you know it, you can find yourself completely disengaged from any relationship with people who don't know Jesus, and you think the more you drown yourself in "Christian" community the more holy you become.

If Jesus taught about reaching the lost, sent His disciples out to continue teaching the ways of God to those who have not embraced it and prays for us now as we continue in the world, what leads us to believe that the Holy Spirit would guide us away from engaging in these things?

How is it possible that we think the more disengaged we are the more spiritually mature we are?

If the Holy Spirit brings to remembrance all that Jesus taught, how did we ever get to the point where we actually believe it's God's will for us to separate in such ways?

Jesus even specifically asked God to *not* take us out of the world (see John 17:15), but instead to sanctify us as we live in it (see vv. 16-17). What does this mean? It simply means that Jesus asked for us to be set apart for God's use as we engage in this world.

Yet, it never ceases to amaze me how we so easily fall into the ways and thinking of the Pharisees. Just like them, we spiritualize separating from everything but the Christian circle we feel is safe.

There is something drastically wrong with this picture.

The Importance of Practical Engagement

Looking back on my Christian infancy, I realize that stepping away from certain people was driven, much more than I'd like to admit, by misunderstanding what Jesus taught and modeled. And, sure, maybe I couldn't be at fault because of my infancy, but I now know differently and must walk carefully.

If you've gotten this far in this book, you should know enough to walk carefully too. There are things you have to separate your-self from. For instance, there is no need to engage in pornography so that you can somehow reach the people who star in the films. But you have to be able to distinguish between separating from things of this nature and the everyday things and people of the world. Just because there are extremes doesn't mean you have to separate from everything. The furthering of the gospel depends on your engagement in the things of the world. In fact, engagement with the world is required.

For instance, in Matthew 5, Jesus calls His followers "the light of the world" (v. 14). He points out that you don't hide the light, but instead you put it in places where it can be seen (see Matt. 5:15). Then he gives us a practical means of how this plays out in everyday life. In verse 16, He says we shine our light into the world *so that* people will see our "good works" and glorify God.

How will they "see" your good deeds if the only way you serve is inside the four walls of your church building?

How will they see the good you are doing if you spend time only with Christians and arrogantly separate yourself from everyone else?

The Bible actually gives us some insight into how much doing good in the world is critical to the furtherance of the gospel and the shining of our light. Paul said that Christ gave Himself up for us "to purify for himself a people for his own possession who are zealous for good works" (Titus 2:14).

So, part of the reason Christ gave Himself up for us was to excite us about doing good! Part of being the "possession" of Christ is to be engaged in doing good.

Paul tells Titus to remind those he leads to "be ready for every good work" (Titus 3:1). He even ties doing good as an appropriate response to our salvation. He talks about how the Holy Spirit has renewed us (see v. 5) through what Christ has done (see v. 6); and he exhorts Titus to insist on these things "so that those who have believed in God may be careful to devote themselves to good works" (v. 8).

In other words, combined with Jesus' statement in Matthew 5, a proper understanding of what the Holy Spirit does and of what Jesus has provided pushes us to do good *in the world*. Worded differently, if we understand the gospel, we will do good.

Paul goes even further with this concept by saying, "And let our people learn to devote themselves to good works, so as to help cases of urgent need, and not be unfruitful" (3:14). Did you see that? If we don't meet needs, we are unfruitful. Wow.

To be in tune with the Holy Spirit and obey our call of furthering the gospel message, we have to engage in doing good. Your good deeds and engagement with the poor and needy is a means of shining your light so that people will glorify God (see Matt. 5:16).

If you move out in such a manner, you can be confident that the Holy Spirit is at work in your life. He does not guide you into separating from the things of the world, but rather to serving those in the world. This is clearly the model Jesus provided us to follow. There is simply no way around it. His modeling didn't make the Pharisees comfortable, but instead exposed how much they had wrongly separated from the people of the world.

If you compare your way of life and the relationships you have with what Jesus modeled, what does this reveal? He was constantly engaged with the very people the most religious people wouldn't even go near.

How many non-Christian people do you know and intentionally stay connected with? If you have a hard time listing names, you have to be honest with yourself. You have fallen into a Pharisaical mentality. You have lost your sense of purpose and have followed the wrong counsels.

Wait; hold on.

Be encouraged.

This is a struggle for all of us.

We naturally gravitate toward others just like us. We feel more comfortable and safe.

Let's collectively thank God that Jesus isn't physically here anymore, because every single one of us desperately needs the Holy Spirit's guidance in this area of our lives!

Comforted in Temptation

One of the reasons people disengage from the world is out of fear of falling into temptation. But we're not talking about hanging out in strip clubs here. We are talking about engaging with those who are in the world.

The bottom line for disengaging from the world is simply evidence that we have listened to the counsel of fear versus faith and have fallen into the mentality of the Pharisees. To not engage in the world for fear of being tempted is to miss an incredible opportunity to show the power of the Holy Spirit in your life. It's to miss the comfort of feeling your Helper at work in your life.

Have you ever noticed what Mark 1:12-13 says? You probably don't know what that verse says without looking it up, so let me set the context real quickly.

Mark starts his book with the fact that the Old Testament has put Jesus on display (see Mark 1:1-3) and he is clear to point out that John the Baptist had spent his life also putting Jesus on display (see vv. 4-8). Mark then describes Jesus' baptism by John (see v. 9) and how God, the Father, puts Him on display as His Son for all who were there to see (see vv. 10-11).

Then the Holy Spirit takes Jesus out into the wilderness . . . catch this . . .

for the purpose of
being personally tempted
by Satan (see vv. 12-13).

Seriously?! Have you ever thought about why the Holy Spirit would intentionally put Jesus in a position where He would be tempted? From our perspective the Holy Spirit would never guide us into a situation where we would be tempted, right?

The Holy Spirit does something amazing here. He puts Jesus on display to the entire demonic world. With the Holy Spirit's power and the ministry of angels (see v. 13), Jesus overcomes the temptation, declaring to the demonic world that the power of the Holy Spirit is greater than their power.

What an opportunity!

What if we viewed times of temptation as a means of putting Jesus on display? What if we viewed temptation as a means to display the power of the Holy Spirit in us? What if, instead of operating in fear of being tempted, we moved out into the world in faith that the Holy Spirit will comfort and guide us through it? Worded differently, what if, instead of disengaging from the world out of fear, we engaged in faith, trusting God to answer Jesus' prayer of protecting and using us as we engage in serving those in the world (see John 17:9-19)?

I'm not talking about sinfully indulging in the things of the world in order to reach those in it. I'm talking about obeying the Holy Spirit's voice that reminds us of and guides us toward embracing the teachings of Jesus. Toward serving people. Toward doing good. Toward finding ways to purposefully build relationships with those outside of our religious circle and intentionally engage with our neighbors that sleep 75 feet from us 365 days a year. We engage
for the purpose of bringing
the gospel into a world
that desperately needs it.

Fear of being defiled will not lead you toward this thinking, and neither will living in fear of other religious people in your life. But the Holy Spirit will.

May we embrace Him and not our religiously driven fears; and may we find a community of people centered and focused on Jesus and His teachings. On that note, let's talk about that type of community in the next chapter; it's the type of community the Holy Spirit will guide you toward.

REFLECTION QUESTIONS

1. What similarities do you see between the content of chapter 1 and this chapter?

2. In what ways do you struggle with the mindset of the Pharisees?

3. How does Jesus' prayer in John 17 change the way you seek answers from God?

4. How does this chapter compare to your previous thoughts on temptation?

5. Do you think this chapter will change what you pray for or pray about? How?

CHAPTER 8

Counseled in Gospel-Centered Community

I work from coffee shops for a couple of reasons. For one, I don't have my own office in our church building. I choose to frequently go to coffee shops because I have no chance of meeting anyone new in the "all-mighty church fortress." I'm not an extreme extrovert, but I do seek to be intentional about meeting people who aren't Christian, and this is one way I can do that on a daily basis. By being out in the community and frequently going to the same places, I get to know people—both employees and regular customers. I have met many people who have become dear friends this way. It's time well spent, I think.

One of the things I've noticed about coffee shops is that they are often the gathering point for community. People have business meetings there. Groups of moms walk there with their children to meet. Men and women gather for Bible studies. And there are groups of people that have met at the coffee shop for a long time and continue to gather at specific times of the day and week to talk and connect with one another.

There is a coffee shop right by my house where I have met a wonderful group of people. They are all older than me; in fact, most of them are retired. By my being around the coffee shop often enough when they gather in the afternoons, they have accepted me into their community. I can show up around 3:00, and before you know it, I'm sitting in a group of six to seven people, talking about any subject under the sun. One thing is certain: There is a lot of laughter with this group. They know I pastor a church, and I have talked about Jesus with many of them. They are wonderful folks, and I genuinely enjoy being around them.

There is another coffee shop close to my house where I have gotten to know a different group of people. I see each of them individually from time to time throughout the week, but the set time to connect with all of them is Friday mornings. Like the first group I mentioned, I got to know them by being around when they gathered. They have also accepted me into their community. The four of us can sit around the fireplace on a Friday and talk about anything from politics to movies to raising children. They are wonderful people that I really enjoy being around and have grown to love.

These communities of people have gotten to know each other, know what's going on in each other's lives and care deeply for one another. They know where they can go if they need to talk to someone or they have something they want to celebrate with others. All people desire to have this type of community. We all want to be connected with a community where we are known and loved, and where we can know others and love them too. We can have community like this at a school, a workplace or with other parents that have kids on the same Little League team. There is no shortage of opportunities to engage in a community of people, but each one begins with a commonality between those within it.

When we bought our house, I obviously didn't know any of the neighbors. But I did know something we all had in common.

We lived in the same neighborhood. We moved in February, and if you know anything about Portland, you know it rains a lot in the winter. So, initially it was tough to meet our neighbors. When summer rolled around, we would see people in passing or out in the yard working. But we wanted to get to know them better; so my wife and I decided to invite everyone to a neighborhood barbecue. It was a fantastic connecting point for those in our neighborhood, and it has become an annual gathering we do every summer.

We have grown to love our neighbors and appreciate each of them so much. We truly feel like we live in a community. It's wonderful.

Every community is centered on something, whether it is a neighborhood, a gathering place or a common goal. Every community has people in it where relationships are built and belonging is found. The question for you and me is not whether we desire community, but what type of community we will pursue.

Regardless of what other types of community we engage, we can be certain God desires us to be a part of a community that is centered on the person of Jesus and focused on furthering the gospel message (see 2 Cor. 5:14-21).

I call this type of community *Gospel-centered*. It's a community of people that collectively seek to know, love, enjoy and proclaim Jesus Christ. I believe this is the type of community God would tell you to be a part of.

A Critical Distinction

We all long to be part of a community because God has wired us as relational beings, and we are designed to function within relationship. Some of us might be more introverted than others and rejuvenate when we are alone. Even so, we still desire to be a part of something greater than ourselves. This is why everyone pursues community at some level. Some are more extroverted and pursue relationship interpersonally, in different facets, while others may only pursue being a part of online communities. Either way, we all seek connection with people we have something in common with.

A gospel community will have many similar characteristics as any other functioning community, but knowing, loving, enjoying and proclaiming Jesus is the common ground for all involved and what makes it distinct.

Practically then, the reasons that people seek it must be different.

Most people enter a community of some sort to meet their own relational needs and desires. But no community of people will function in a healthy manner if everyone is there to meet their own best interests. When everyone seeks to consume community, nobody ends up getting it. If they do, it's only because there are a few in the community who either feed off being needed by others, are people pleasers or maybe are just humble and selfless. These few inevitably exhaust themselves, which hinders the longevity of these communities for two reasons. They burn out people who are seeking to help others, and the people who enter a community as consumers never end up getting what they want. These two things inevitably cause the community to break down.

Now, some people need more investment than others. As a pastor, I totally get that. But when it comes to engaging in a gospel community, it requires the majority of those in it to operate differently. It can sustain a few "consumers" who just need time and patience. But the majority of people have to embrace the gospel in practical ways, denying themselves and seeking to give community to others. The amazing thing is that when the majority of people in the community are seeking to *give* community to others, everyone ends up *getting* it as well (see Acts 2:42-47)!

It works backward from the normal human pattern. Living out the gospel tends to do that. We have to fight our natural tendency to look out for ourselves. This is as practical as it gets when it comes to staying in step with the Holy Spirit's voice and counsel in your life. The Holy Spirit will guide you toward giving community to others and serving others because that's what Jesus taught and modeled for us (see Matt. 20:25-28).

The Holy Spirit reminds us of these things and guides us toward them.

So, the critical distinction of gospel community is that it is made up of a group of people seeking to know, love, enjoy and proclaim Jesus. One of the ways this can be embraced in a practical way is to pursue *giving* community. Now, a few questions for you.

How does this compare with your motivation for engaging in community?

Would you say you are more a consumer of community or a giver of it?

Do you look for people who need community, or do you only tend to find people you are already in community with?

Do you seek giving community because you like to feel needed, or because you love God and are seeking to love people? That's a question you may need to wrestle with a bit. There are no right or wrong answers here. It's simply about recognizing where you are.

And wherever that is, you need the Holy Spirit to keep you in step with Him. We all do, which is why we are better off without Jesus' physical presence.

The crazy thing is, as we discussed in the last chapter, we are not just called to serve other Christians, but also to serve those in the world. All of a sudden we realize that our lives cannot be about us anymore if we are following the voice of the Holy Spirit. Looking at the call of the gospel to continually focus on others might make some feel burdened. But I can tell you that when I am serving others out of my love for God and people, it's anything but burdensome. When I am seeking to give community to others with love as my motivator, I am actually energized. Not drained. Jesus says His burden is light (see Matt. 11:30). It only becomes heavy when we seek to serve and give out of duty and legalism versus love.

When we are growing in our knowledge of Jesus, loving and enjoying Him, we seek to proclaim Him as well. And we do this with much more than words. We do it by following His lifestyle example of servanthood. And it's this attitude that makes gospel-community so much fun to be a part of.

If you are in tune with the Holy Spirit's counsel, you will move toward engaging in a gospel community like this. By *engaging*, I mean being a part of, contributing to, a community like this and possibly even initiating it yourself.

God's Means Toward Maturity

I talk to people all the time who question what it means to be *the* Church. They question everything from leadership structures to theology to what "church" is supposed to be like. This process of evaluation can be very healthy, but we have to at least make sure we understand that ongoing connection with the people of God is vital for anyone desiring to follow the Holy Spirit's leading in his or her life.

The apostle Paul offers us, in Ephesians 4:1-16, some amazing insights into this process. This section of Scripture makes it clear that we have been given unity in Christ and we have to be diligent to preserve it (see Eph. 4:3). Many people think about having to build unity with other Christians, but we have already been given unity! We just have to maintain it. Paul also makes it clear that we are one body with one Spirit (see v. 4) and we are under one God (see v. 6) that has graciously gifted people (see vv. 7-8).

"Spiritual gifts" are often applied wrongly in the American Church. They are often viewed selfishly. We think about them through the lens of what we are good at or the skills we personally possess. Whether we realize it or not, this makes the gifts about us. But that understanding misses the very core of their design and leads us away from embracing the gospel. These spiritual gifts aren't about what we are capable of doing; they are about how God uses us in the lives of other people.

In other words, the gifts we possess point to God's grace, and not to our abilities.

Paul explains how gifts are given for the "building up [of] the body of Christ" (see v. 12). The gifts are given to people for the benefit of the whole Body, not just to the one possessing the gift. These gifts are given for the purpose of unifying Christians to become mature in their faith, until they reach the "stature of the fullness of Christ" (v. 13). Practically speaking, we know we are getting to that point when we won't give way to false and deceitful teachings (see v. 14). Worded differently, we are stepping in that direction when we embrace the truth of Jesus.

In this context we see a beautiful description of how gospel community practically works itself out. Paul says the Body of Christ is joined and held together by what *every* joint supplies . . . and when "each part is working properly" the Body of Christ lovingly "builds itself up" (v. 16).

That is a beautiful description of gospel-community. Everyone has gifts (see Rom. 12:6-13), and those gifts, *when* they are used in the lives of others, lead to the Body of Christ being built up. That means the exercising of your gift builds up other people.

Now that's how community ought to work! So, you see, if every person pursued community as a consumer, none of this would happen. On the other hand, when we pursue community as a Christ follower, as people who seek to deny ourselves daily and serve others, we can accomplish what we are designed to accomplish. It is when we view everything in light of the gospel that we are in tune with the Spirit's voice in our lives and we feel His presence.

If you are struggling to see God at work in your life, try pursuing community with this gospel focus. What you will find is the Holy Spirit leading you in that direction, comforting you in ways that are unexplainable and then energizing you as you seek to embrace the teachings of Jesus. In fact, if you do these things, it is evidence that the Holy Spirit is at work in your life because there is nothing in and of yourself that would lead you to those ends. If you try to muster up enough strength by your own efforts, your experience will be exhausting. Love for God and people must be your motivator. When it is, your engagement in gospel-community will be beneficial and exhilarating for everyone involved.

Markers of Gospel-Communities

At Colossae Church, we have labored to articulate some outcomes we desire to see in our gospel-communities. Our list is not exhaustive but simply serves us as markers or evidences of people being led by the Holy Spirit in and through gospel-community. I will walk through these markers with the hope of your seeing these as checkpoints for yourself as well.

Before I do, I want to make it clear that these are not *the* markers, but simply some that help us see how the Holy Spirit is at work within the people of the community. No community operates perfectly, but we do know that gospel-community will function best when the people in it are in tune with the Holy Spirit and thus striving to do these things:

They operate out of a love for God. Gospel-community is made up of people seeking to love God with everything within them (see Matt. 22:37-39); and that alone serves as their motivator for engagement.

They truly love others within the community. Jesus says that our love for one another is how the world will know that we are His people (see John 13:34-35). If people are loving toward one another, they will be patient and kind with one another; they won't be arrogant and boastful; they won't insist on their own way; they won't be irritated by one another; but instead, they will rejoice in the truths of Jesus and will continue in patterns of doing these things (see 1 Cor. 13:4-7).

They protect unity in the midst of diversity. Gospel-community is at work when the people within it value each other's differences (see 1 Cor. 12:12) and pursue each other in a humble manner that leads toward a unity of mindset (see 1 Pet. 3:8). When a community is lovingly operating in these ways, they can be confident that God is with them (see 2 Cor. 13:11).

They initiate relationships with one another outside of organized events. People engaging in gospel-community are pursuing connection with one another outside of structures put in place by leadership (see Rom. 15:5-7). They live their lives with one another; being a part of organized things on a church campus is only a part of that (see Acts 2:46-47).

They embrace the call to disciple others. A gospel-community is made up of people who, as they go about the nuances of their lives, are embracing the call to make disciples (see Matt. 28:18-20). And if each part is working properly, the community will be filled with people who are mutually encouraging one another (see Rom. 1:11-12).

They live out what they already know. To be an active participant in a gospel-community, people must seek to embrace what they already know. It's one thing to sit around and theorize about ideologies or talk about the distinctions between different theological thoughts. It's another to actually be a "doer" of the things you know are true (see Jas. 1:22). Gospel-communities are made up of people who are seeking to embrace what they know and are learning more as they do so.

They have a mindset of servanthood. These communities are filled with people who serve one another, making sure nobody is living with unmet needs (see Acts 2:44-45), and they are also seeking to serve the poor and needy of the world (see Titus 3:14). At Colossae Church, we talk about this as us having a balance between being the "Body to the Body" and the "Body to the world." Gospel-communities are seeking to be balanced in these two things. And by keeping this balance, they are giving an accurate proclamation of the gospel. If the community loses one side of this balance, they lose that proclamation. It must be in both word and deed.

They value every spiritual gift. A gospel-community is working properly when every gift is viewed as necessary for the overall health of the people in it (see 1 Cor. 12:4-7). Gospel-communities function best when each person knows how God uses him or her in the lives of the others and can actually be used in that way (see Rom. 12:6-13).

They take responsibility for their own spiritual growth. When people take ownership for growing in their knowledge of God, gospel-community is going to work at its best (see Heb. 5:11-14). Far too often people want everything to be done and provided for them. They want their study of Scripture to be structured by someone else. If it's not provided for them, they get frustrated. In most cases, these are people who look to church leadership to structure everything for them; and without this, they assume they can't grow in their relationship with God. Leadership has a certain amount of responsibility to shepherd the people God has given them (see 1 Pet. 5:1-2), but enabling a consumer mentality isn't ultimately beneficial. There must be a balance here, and gospel-community is at work when the members of it encourage one another toward Christlikeness outside of any formal structure put in place by leadership (see Heb. 3:12-14).

They seek the benefit of accountability. True and holistic accountability happens when a variety of people see us in the context of everyday life with our friends, spouses, kids. We can gather apart from our spouse and children and roommates once a week with a group of guys or women and call it "accountability," but this is not true accountability. It's disclosure. This type of gathering is a place where you can go and disclose what you want others to know about you. You can then leave and go back to your life. This type of setting can be beneficial, but it's not holistic accountability in and of itself. If those in a gospel-community have a disclosure group, they also embrace the beauty of holistic accountability. They live life with people who can see every aspect of their lives, and they do so because they want to be held accountable for their pursuit of Christ. They want to make sure they don't operate one way around certain types of people and another way around others (see Gal. 2:11-14). And they willingly accept any sort of discipline action that may come when they are straying off course (see Matt. 18:15-17).

People engaged in gospel-community humbly embrace these things. Or at least they try as they prayerfully ask the help of the Holy Spirit.

Gospel Community and Spiritual Leadership

If you are trying to embrace these types of characteristics, you can be certain your Helper is at work in your life. And I would argue that it's a community such as this the Holy Spirit would guide you toward. If you find yourself in a place of not living out the things I mentioned above, my encouragement would be for you to ask the Holy Spirit to lead you into these types of lifestyle choices.

Because you love God.

Because you desire to be in step with the gospel, today.

These lifestyle characteristics are not necessarily natural for us to live out, which is why we can celebrate the fact that the Holy Spirit is not limited by physical presence. We all need His help in these areas.

One lesson I've learned in this regard is that God uses spiritual leaders to guide us toward embracing these things. I am personally thankful for the spiritual leaders God has placed me under. There is much discussion about how leaders have abused their authoritative position, and this has led some people to think that any form of positional authority in a church context is wrong. But this is simply a reaction that swings the pendulum too far the other direction. Just because some have sinfully abused their

God-given position of authority doesn't mean we should forgo God's design of the local church.

In fact, the Scriptures make it clear that leadership is necessary. Although Jesus spoke against the areas in which the religious leaders of His day were off base and abusing their authority (for example, see Mark 7:9-13), He never spoke against formal structures of leadership.

The New Testament shows examples of how faithful people were pleased to have godly leaders over them (for instance, see Acts 6:1-7). We know that we are to have leaders who oversee local bodies of people (see 1 Pet. 5:1-2; Titus 1:5-9; 1 Tim. 3:1-13) and that we are supposed to submit to those placed over us in leadership (see Heb. 13:7,17).

I take this personally. I am the founding pastor of Colossae Church, and I also serve as an elder. But make no mistake, I am clearly *under* the authority of the other elders in our church. I submit to them and believe this is God-honoring. God gives some people positions of leadership, but He also places everyone under leadership.

When I was in the midst of the fraud situation, I had to embrace this truth at very personal levels. The elders I was submitting to had to make a lot of decisions that directly affected me. From the "outside," I didn't understand some of their decisions because I didn't know all the reasoning behind them. This is where bitterness can creep in very, very easily.

This is when I had to fall in line with the Holy Spirit in practical ways. I had to submit to and support my leaders; and as I did so, I had to make sure I avoided any feelings of bitterness (see Heb. 12:7-17). I also had to maintain unity. If I talked to people, I had to maintain that. I could not go around talking to everyone else about what I didn't understand. When people talk about what they don't understand, it *only* creates disunity. I had to recognize that God had placed them over me and He was going to use them to teach me lessons I needed to learn. These were not just decisions my leaders were making; these were circumstances God was orchestrating to teach me.

That is a truth to get excited about!

The Holy Spirit led me to realize that God was disciplining me to be more like Jesus and using those in leadership over me to lead me to that end. Just because I didn't understand every nuance didn't mean God wasn't in it. I never understand everything He's doing anyway. Why, then, would I assume that I needed to know everything in this situation?

It was through the guidance of my Helper that I recognized how God uses those over us to teach us lessons we would otherwise miss. Being frustrated because I didn't know every nuance of the decision-making process in my circumstances could have led me to become bitter; but being a part of the Body of Christ means that I trusted God to speak to me through my leaders. By following His lead in this, I experienced the Holy Spirit's work in my life like no other time. It wasn't necessarily in my timing, and it wasn't always easy. But He comforted me in the midst of these times; and through submitting, I learned invaluable lessons. They were so invaluable, in fact, that it made losing all that money worth it.

If you desire to be a part of a gospel-community, you must also embrace the benefit of accountability. That includes the submission to the leaders God places over you. He holds them accountable for how they lead you and holds you accountable to follow their lead (see Heb. 13:17).

I am ending this chapter with this point simply because too many people are becoming disgruntled with their church leaders. They look at the things I've written about in this chapter and, out of idealism, hold them up as a standard for churches, assuming that every person should embrace every value perfectly, today.

This is nothing less than arrogance. If they are honest with themselves, they will quickly recognize that they don't uphold all these things perfectly either.

The bottom line is that anyone who is engaged with a local church body will quickly realize its imperfections. That's because it's filled with imperfect people. But the Holy Spirit is at work and will accomplish (complete) the work He has begun (see Phil. 1:6). For that reason alone it's worth sticking it out and helping the church body you are a part of work toward God's design.

The Counselor will guide you toward preserving unity in the Body of Christ. God might lead you to go to another church, but I would earnestly exhort you to first consider the possibility that He wants you to remain in your current context *so that* He can teach you some things. Maybe, just maybe, the Counselor is guiding you toward living out your faith in that context . . . humbly . . . patiently . . . trusting that He is at work in everyone involved. Including you.

May we all consider the reality that we have things to learn.

REFLECTION QUESTIONS

1. Have you ever viewed "community" as something you can give, rather than just receive? How do you think this idea could change what you pray for?

2. Does this chapter change your perspective of being involved in church at all? How?

3. Which markers of gospel-community do you possess? Which markers do you need to ask God to help you with?

4. How can you be a part of cultivating these markers in your church context?

CHAPTER 9

Comforted in Steps of Growth

Everyone used to tell me that being a parent was going to be more work than I imagined. That has certainly proven to be true, at many levels. But nobody ever told me that being a parent would bring more joy than I ever thought.

I still remember the first time I saw Karis's little face. I was completely overcome with emotion, and I remember tears streaming down my face. The joy within me at that moment was beyond any amount of vocabulary to verbally express.

I also remember the first time I saw Hope's face. The same emotions rose within me, and I remember thinking how amazing it was to have yet another little girl to raise and teach and disciple. And the same thing happened when Sayla was born. The amount of joy was immeasurable.

I didn't grow up imagining myself having three daughters, but today I, of course, can't imagine not having them. I do tell people that parenting will be more work than they think, but I also tell them to expect more joy.

On this morning I am writing this, my girls are seven, four and eight weeks old. Watching a little child grow up is absolutely amazing. When a child goes from lying flat on his or her back to being able to roll over, it's a wonderful time.

We're amazed at the progression. We celebrate with laughter and clapping. We call our spouse into the room so they could see for themselves. When the grandparents ask how the baby is doing, we are excited to share about the growth and steps.

Then the baby gets to the point where he or she scoots or rolls over multiple times just to get a little toy. We begin to move the toys a little farther away from them so that we can enjoy their new abilities.

When babies go from being on their hands and knees and rocking back and forth to actually crawling, we smile and are amazed at how fast they're getting around and growing up.

Next thing you know, they are grabbing onto the edge of the couch and pulling themselves up, standing on their own two feet while bouncing up and down.

We smile and enjoy the look of accomplishment on our baby's face in each of these stages. These are wonderful moments as a parent.

I remember the first steps Karis took. I think she was able to take two steps before plopping back down on her backside. At that moment, Barbara and I looked at each other with smiles from ear to ear, clapping and cheering her on. It was the first time she took a step, and the fact that she even tried deserved celebration. These were big steps for her, and for us as parents too.

It's in moments of progression and growth that we celebrate.

Here is my point: When Karis took her first two steps, I didn't step back in frustration, wishing she had taken four.

It's all a process of growing up; and every step of growth taken today is critical for the ones that follow. Recognition of the letters of the alphabet comes before sounding out the letters; and sounding them out comes before reading words. Life is filled with these types of examples. Everything we do as adults is based on the little steps we first took as children.

The same is true with our spiritual lives and can be said about our ability to hear God speak to us and recognize when He is at work in us, or moving us on to something else.

Throughout this book, I have articulated some ways that we can be confident we are hearing God's voice, and it really comes down to our thinking. But all of that can be quite overwhelming when viewed at one glance. Sure, for some people the pages prior to this might seem elementary in some ways. But perhaps for you it's been the opposite. Maybe you've been challenged in some areas and are actually a little overwhelmed.

I want to encourage you. The basic truths of the gospel may be simple to understand, but fully embracing them does not come easy for any of us. I've written about what I have obviously thought a lot about.

And it's still hard.

We have to be disciplined and intentional.

We desire to be further along than we are, but we must trust the Holy Spirit to bring us along one step at a time (see Phil. 1:6).

We all have growing up to do (see 2 Pet. 3:18).

The Necessity of Time

The home my family and I were living in prior to moving to Portland had rose bushes in the front yard. I never really understood how to care for them properly. I was never told when I was supposed to prune them or exactly how much water they should get. But over time, I eventually learned enough to at least keep them alive.

I mostly learned this by killing rose bushes and almost killing others. I picked up some tips by reading about roses online and trying different things based on what my friends with rose bushes told me they had learned. It took some time to learn what not to do, but eventually, I figured it out.

If I were to invest more time in understanding rose bushes and actually caring for them, I'm sure I could eventually know enough to start a nursery. With enough time, I guess, we could do just about anything well. It may not be worth investing so much time into caring for rose bushes, but over time, caring for them would probably be like second nature.

It's like riding a bike. At first it's difficult to avoid falling down. But before you know it, you're riding without even thinking about it. You suddenly become aware that you are doing things subconsciously that you didn't even know you had to do before.

It's like driving a car. Most of us never realize how much we know and understand until we begin teaching someone else. Then it hits us how much we are doing by intuition without thinking about it. And we realize the 15-year-old who got her permit yesterday doesn't understand any of that! It's in these moments we wish that the imaginary brake we are pushing on the passenger-side floorboard actually worked.

I had some friends from Romania visiting, and they had never watched an American football game. I was explaining the rules to them one down at a time. To me it all seemed pretty simple; but after about 10 minutes, my friends were completely overwhelmed by all the rules. I realized that the years I had invested in playing and understanding football had simplified all the complexities. I forgot how much I knew and how much I had learned.

Everything takes time; but as we invest more time, we learn and grow. This truth applies to learning how to more accurately incline your ear to hear God's voice and drown out the other counsels in your life. It applies to allowing your Helper to lead you to embrace all that Jesus taught. It all takes time. You will go through ups and downs, do some things right and make some mistakes. It's all a process, but your Helper will, in fact, teach you.

I remember one time when I was in the front yard with Karis and she was looking at the rose bushes. I was standing close to her, watching to make sure she didn't get pricked. But she was very interested in the bright red flowers and simply couldn't resist reaching out to grab the branch. Like any loving father would, I intercepted her hand and said, "No, no, baby. That will give you an owie." It was at this moment her bottom lip began to curl outward and she looked at me with tear-filled eyes.

She had looked at and smelled flowers all the time, so she obviously didn't understand why I wouldn't let her touch the branch. Why, all of a sudden, couldn't she touch and smell this one?

She then took her eyes off me and looked back at the rose bush. With a little look of determination, she slowly began to stretch out her hand to grab hold of it. She did this partly out of her spite and rebellion, but I also think at least in part she was legitimately confused as to why she couldn't do it.

I again intercepted her hand. She cried again.

Kneeling down to her level, I gently let her hand down and told her to be careful because the bush could really hurt her.

We repeated this process one more time. After the third interception when I placed her hand down, she barely waited three seconds before raising her hand again to grab the bush. Determined little girl.

Set on getting to the bush, this time she thrust her hand out as fast as she could to grab it. What she didn't realize was that this time I had already decided I wasn't going to stop her.

After grabbing it, she very quickly realized why I wasn't allowing her to. She not only grabbed the branch, but squeezed it. She immediately began to cry. She opened her hand and saw blood and quickly buried her head into my chest. After a minute or so, I asked her to show me her "owies." When she held out her arm there were scrapes up to her elbow and two small holes in the palm of her hand with blood coming out of them.

A sad moment as a father, but one that I knew was ultimately beneficial for her. Because of that experience, she never again reached out to grab a rose bush. In fact, at times she would ask me if she could touch any of the flowers we would see. She had learned a valuable lesson. Over the course of time, she will come to understand more and more about life, the things that will hurt her and those things that won't. I can do my best to tell her before they happen, but the truth is, she will probably choose to learn things through her own experiences.

You gain experience over time. I want to encourage you to continue embracing the simple truths we have discussed so far in this book and by doing so you will gain needed experience. You will grow in your confidence and ability to hear God speak. You will become more confident in your ability to listen to God's direction. And you will find yourself more quickly realizing which directions are clearly *not* from God.

I'm no expert, and I obviously don't have a magic formula, but I am growing more sensitive to His direction and voice every day. And a lot through mistakes.

Just as I have and will continue to do, you will also grab hold of some things along the way that will cause you pain, and you will kill some rose bushes; but through it all, you will learn invaluable lessons. Regardless of where you are in your faith today, you can and should get to the point where things that used to baffle your mind will suddenly come naturally. Walking in the Holy Spirit, with and by the Holy Spirit, can be second nature to you. You won't stress over decisions as much as you will enjoy walking with God through them.

And perhaps another benefit about your gained experience is that you will also be able to offer others much-needed grace as they fall after taking their first steps (see Jas. 3:1-2). Because you have been there, you will celebrate their two steps and cheer them on toward taking two more.

This joy and grace will come, but you must make one critical distinction to get there.

From Theological Points to Personal Encounter

When I first became a Christian, I really wanted to absorb as much as I could about the Bible and its teachings. I was reading and reading and reading, and continually excited about all I was learning. I underlined and highlighted. I had a list of questions I compiled during my times of reading and was asking anyone who knew more than me to help me find answers.

In fact, I went to Bible college because I wanted to learn more about the Bible. I didn't go because I wanted to be in ministry. I went with the agenda of growing in my faith.

I decided to take it to this level of education after I volunteered to help out as a counselor at a junior high summer camp. The church I was attending at the time went to a camp every year; at the last minute, they needed another warm-blooded, breathing person to be a guys' cabin leader. I had been a Christian for about three months at the time and had never been to a camp, so I had no idea what I was getting myself into. But I jumped on the opportunity to help out.

I remember going to the chapel twice a day, and each time being blown away at how much I was learning. I may have been a little embarrassed by how little I knew, but mostly I just realized I had a lot to learn.

A few of the kids in my cabin knew the books of the Bible and could recite them in order. They were having contests all week to see who could recite them all correctly and the fastest. If I was lucky, I could have probably named a dozen; but obviously in random order, and I probably wouldn't have been able to tell you if they were Old or New Testament books. I didn't grow up in church, so even though these boys were much younger than I was, they had spent much more time in this Christian "world" than I had.

A few of the kids talked about stories in the Old Testament as if they were common knowledge to everyone alive, but I had no clue what they were talking about or even if the stories were actually in Scripture.

Kids talked about Michael W. Smith songs, and I actually thought they were talking about George Michael. He had a song called "Faith," so it made sense to me.

I'm dead serious. I honestly thought that was who they were talking about and they were saying his name wrong. I laughed inside, thinking they were so cute.

There was so much I didn't know about Christian subculture or about the Scriptures or about God, Jesus and the Holy Spirit. All I knew was that I believed in Jesus, and the Bible was where I learned about Him. I was an infant taking my first two steps.

In Bible college, I began to learn a lot about Scripture and was amazed by some of the controversies surrounding its origin and preservation. I learned about God and Jesus and the Holy Spirit and some of the different theological thoughts people hold within Christian circles. I took classes on how to study the Scriptures accurately. I learned about Paul's missionary journeys and studied some books of the Bible in depth. I took all the theology classes. I was soaking in as much information as I could.

I felt like I was growing in my faith. I was, kind of.

Even though I was filling my mind with all this great information, I still was left wondering about the practicalities of all I was learning. I still felt like I was missing something but couldn't put my finger on it.

Gaining this information was ultimately very helpful for me. I wanted to learn, and I was thankful for those who were teaching me sound doctrine (see Titus 2:1). The more I read Scripture the more quickly I was able to grasp what I was reading. This is one way in which I grew in confidence that the Holy Spirit was speaking to me. The whole theological idea of "illumination" is that when we understand something we read in Scripture it's because the Holy Spirit allowed us to see it.

That's a simple and straightforward way you can gain confidence in your ability to hear God speak to you too. When you read something that you have read dozens of times before, but all of a sudden the truth of that verse hits you, that's the Holy Spirit speaking and teaching you! When that happens you should take a moment and thank Him for helping you. He is guiding you and teaching you. He is at work in your life.

Recognizing that is vital to your Christian walk.

But regardless of how much information we have, we must also embrace it in practical ways.

It's through my understanding of what the Scriptures are saying that has led me to make the points I have in this book. I have referenced many different Scriptures to provide some backbone to the points I have made, and I really hope you have taken the time to look up some of them and compare them to what you have read in Scripture (see Acts 17:11).

But you have to make sure you don't confuse theological information with the truth.

Let me explain this distinction a little more.

Early on in my faith, I thought learning about truth was about obtaining more information. I wanted to learn more about the Bible, which is obviously a great thing. But the harsh reality was that my pursuit of information quickly made Jesus impersonal.

He was somebody I was learning more and more about instead of someone I was personally becoming closer to.

This may be a fine line, but it's a very big difference and a critical distinction to make if you are to take steps toward Christian maturity.

I missed the fact that embracing truth is about knowing the person of Jesus, not just being able to articulate theologically correct points.

The truth is a Person (see John 14:6), not theological information or a certain set of intellectual beliefs. The moment we confuse that is the moment we have mistaken the voice of the Holy Spirit for another's.

Keeping It Personal

We learn about Jesus (the truth) through the Scriptures; and through them the Holy Spirit leads us to a deeper intimacy with the person of Jesus. That said, I'm going to make what could be somewhat of a controversial statement in some circles, but if it initially rubs you the wrong way, please take a few minutes to think about it further.

Here is the statement: There might be a point where you need to take a step back from obtaining more information about the Bible and about God. Instead, you might consider taking some time to actually seek experiences where you can embrace what you already know. You might want to take a step back and give yourself space to try to actually live out your theology in everyday life. Ask the Holy Spirit to use the information you already have to guide you toward a deeper intimacy with the person of Jesus.

Wisdom isn't gained through obtaining new information alone, but instead by living out the information we have already obtained.

And wisdom would lead you to pursue Jesus personally.

If you still struggle with confidence in your ability to hear God speak to you, learning more information might help you. But be careful that you don't get all this twisted.

Keep it simple and seek to embrace the basic call of the gospel as we have talked about.

Most of the time we get confused because we make things more difficult than they need to be. Gaining more information without embracing the practicalities of what we learn can often contribute to that confusion. We love to talk about the authority of Scripture in our lives, but if we accept its authority we also have to embrace the practicalities of it. The Spirit of truth is not the same as the spirit of intellectualism. The Trinity is not Father, Son and Holy Bible.

When our desire for truth is about gaining head knowledge about the Bible, we lose sight of perhaps the most important truth of Christianity.

Truth is a Person.

The Holy Spirit is a person, and He will guide you to a Person; and to do so, He may use intellectual knowledge to do that. But make no mistake. He is not guiding you *to* information. He is using information to guide you toward Himself.

The Spirit will remind you of the points Jesus made, but only because they will help you know Him more intimately. And that is not just a matter of semantics. It's an important distinction we must all make at some point.

The more you embrace the teachings of Jesus, the more intimate you feel the comforting personal presence of the Holy Spirit in your life. Gaining head knowledge about Him or about the Scriptures alone doesn't lead you toward intimacy. It leads you to arrogance (see 1 Cor. 8:1).

Unfortunately, my pursuit of information early on in my faith got in the way of getting to know Jesus personally. The Holy Spirit is a person and is actually the Spirit of Christ (see 1 Pet. 1:10-11; 1 John 4:13). Just knowing *about* Him leads to arrogance (see 1 Cor. 8:1). Knowing Him personally leads us toward humility (see 1 Pet. 5:5).

I thought that because I could regurgitate more and more information, I was becoming more and more mature in my faith. But the reality was that I just sounded more mature. I knew a bunch of information, but I eventually realized I was actually moving away from personally experiencing Christ in my life.

If I can encourage you in a direction, it would be to make this distinction as early on in your growth process as possible. You may need to learn the hard way by yourself and end up in a place where you feel spiritually dry, feel like you know it all and are bored when you hear something taught that you already "know." But if my process can help you avoid this arrogant posture, I would be ever so grateful.

Growing spiritually is about growing closer to and becoming more like Jesus. In your pursuit of Him, you will learn a lot. But don't lose sight of the Person you are pursuing.

I believe Jesus indirectly drives this point home in John 8:31-32.

Jesus says, "If you abide in my word, you are truly my disciples, and you will know the truth, and the truth will set you free." Jesus begins by making it clear that *if* we remain in His word, we will truly be His disciples. It's conditional.

Then He says that remaining in His word will also result in our coming to "know the truth." The word Jesus uses here is *ginosko*. This is not the word for informational knowledge, but of experiential knowledge. If He wanted to say that they would simply have an informational knowledge of His Word, then He would have used the root word *oida*. However, Jesus is saying that staying true to His Word would lead to experiencing the truth, not just knowing it intellectually. And since we know Jesus is the truth (see John 14:26), we can then say we would be experiencing the person of Jesus, not just knowing *about* Him.

Information about Jesus doesn't set you free. Jesus, Himself, does that.

Information can lead you to Jesus (see Rom. 10:17), but when it does you will personally experience the person of Jesus. It's liberated living. It's freeing.

If you are newer to your faith, let me encourage you a bit here. Please know that people in all stages of their faith struggle with balancing this and can easily confuse personally knowing Jesus with just knowing about Him.

Please be intentional about asking the Holy Spirit to help you avoid that pitfall.

Ask Him to comfort you in your growing process, knowing that you have not lost sight of the person of Jesus. Ask Him to comfort you in your first steps.

In Matthew 7:23, Jesus looked at a group of people and said probably the most frightening statement I know of in Scripture. This group of people knew a lot of information and even did a lot in the name of Jesus, but they missed the point of the information. Jesus tells them that there will be many people who know and say the right things and even do the right things. But in the end, He will say to them, "I never knew you; depart from me, you workers of lawlessness."

Jesus isn't saying He didn't know *about* them. If He wanted to say that, He would have used the word *oida,* which speaks of informational knowledge. Instead He uses the experiential word (*ginosko*), as we just discussed. He says he will tell many people, even though they said and even did some of the right things in the name of Jesus, to "depart" from Him because He didn't have an experiential knowledge of them.

They gave Him lip service, but their hearts were far from Him (see Mark 7:6-7).

Jesus, through the presence of the Holy Spirit, is personal. He isn't a figurehead we just learn more about. He is a person we love with all our heart, soul and mind (see Matt. 22:37-38). And the more we love Him, the more we engage in what He is doing through His Spirit.

Let the Holy Spirit comfort you in your steps of growth toward an experiential and loving knowledge of Jesus. True experience with Jesus will always be grounded in true information, but we must recognize that truth is personal and relational because the truth is a Person.

You may not fully understand or grasp this concept right now, or know how to go about pursuing the person of Jesus. That's okay; we all have to start somewhere, and we all need to be continually helped by the Holy Spirit in our steps of growth. This is yet another way we can individually embrace our Helper in very practical ways. We all need Him to help and comfort us, to teach us to love Him and others more—which is why we truly are better off without Jesus by our side.

REFLECTION QUESTIONS

1. What is most overwhelming to you about trying to listen to God? What insecurities still seem to take over within you?

2. What do you think about the distinction between theological information and truth? How does this compare to what you have assumed up to this point?

3. Do you tend to struggle with intimacy with Jesus or struggle the other direction, lacking in your understanding of Scripture?

4. What do you think about the statement "The more you embrace the teachings of Jesus, the more intimate you feel the comforting personal presence of the Holy Spirit in your life"?

5. How does the statement "Information about Jesus doesn't set you free. Jesus, Himself, does that" affect your view of the Christian life?

CHAPTER 10

A Collective Obedience

It's easy to say that we will do whatever God wants us to do or go wherever God wants us to go. But it's an entirely different thing to actually embrace it. It's much easier to sit around thinking about what God would have us do in a month or year from now than to embrace what He has already told us to do today.

We all know that.

Unfortunately, the saying "I'll do whatever God tells me to do" has become more of a figure of speech than a literal statement. It's like we use the word "butt." I'm not trying to be crude here, but this is the best word I can find to illustrate this point. Think about it. We use this word figuratively all the time.

We sweat our butt off.

We work our butt off.

We freeze it off.

We laugh it off.

We get into fights and kick it.

Or get it kicked.

Adults engage in bets and lose it.

We use the word all the time in ways we don't actually mean. We all know what we are trying to say, but we also know we don't literally embrace the actual words we are using. And we don't expect others to either.

Saying we want to do what God wants us to do cannot be something we say as a figure of speech. It has to be something we actually embrace. And I would argue that it's something we expect others to take literally too.

If we say we will do whatever He wants in a year from now, then we must also do it today. If we are not seeking to do what we already know, then what makes us think we will actually do whatever *that thing* is at a later date?

There always seems to be something that comes before following Jesus today.

Luke 9:57-62 gives us some insight into three men who said they would follow Jesus. The assumption after reading this passage is that none of them actually did. They each had something they needed to do first or that they weren't willing to give up quite yet.

One man says to Jesus, "I will follow you wherever you go" (Luke 9:57).

Jesus replies with the idea that He doesn't have a plan of where He is even going to sleep. That thing called a home, yeah, well, He isn't going to be staying in one of those soon. We can assume the guy didn't follow Jesus. He wasn't willing to set aside his known comforts to follow Jesus quite yet.

Jesus then looks at another guy standing nearby and says, "Follow me."

This guy says, "Lord, let me first go and bury my father" (v. 59). I love how this guy acknowledged Jesus as Lord. The problem was that he had something to do before he would actually follow Jesus. In this culture, this man's dad was likely dead, but there was a waiting period before the body would be buried and the inheritance handed over to him. So this man's issue was money. Once he had all his finances in order, he would follow.

Jesus tells him to let the dead "bury their own dead" (v. 60). Rather than allowing this man to feel good about saying some day he would actually follow Him, Jesus tells him to do so today and immediately "go and proclaim the kingdom of God" (v. 60). The passage implies that this man did not actually follow Jesus either.

Another guy standing there looks at Jesus and says, "I will follow you, Lord, but let me first say farewell to those at my home" (v. 61). This man also acknowledges who Jesus is and simply wanted to say goodbye to his family before following Jesus.

But in Jesus' mind, there is no such thing as a "but first." When Jesus says to follow Him, He means today. He knows that if these guys would not follow Him today, they wouldn't follow Him later either. There would always be a "but first" in their life. There would always be an excuse. Always something else to get through or past before they followed through with His words "Follow me."

This is why Jesus says to this man, "No one who puts his hand to the plow and looks back is fit for the kingdom of God" (v. 62). In other words, if he was serious about following Jesus later, he wouldn't be looking back today. He would be focused on what was ahead rather than looking back at what he was leaving behind.

We can always find "but firsts" in our lives. We can always find an excuse as to why we don't follow today. We can try to avoid actually having to follow and do so while continuing to say we want to do what God wants. It's more like a figure of speech. It sounds good, and we feel spiritual. But we never end up actually embracing what we say.

"Let me just get past the wedding, and then . . ."

"Let me just get past this busy time at work, and then . . ."

"Things in my family are just crazy right now, let me get past this, and then . . ."

"I will follow, but first let me . . . and then I'll . . ."

"I will do whatever God wants. I'm just waiting for Him to make it known, and then . . ."

The sad reality is "and then" rarely, if ever, comes.

Saying these phrases will hinder you from actually following the Holy Spirit's leading in your life. Don't fall into that way of thinking. If you do, there will always be something that hinders you from getting out and joining in with all that God is doing.

Your "and then" never comes because you will simply find another "but first."

The Holy Spirit will always tell you to follow *today*. It is another counsel that is telling you the "but first"s are appropriate. If we are interested in hearing the Holy Spirit's voice, then we must begin by setting our own desires aside, adjusting our schedules and priorities *so that* we can step forward in obedience today.

First Things First

At the end of December 2007, I was speaking at Cornerstone Community Church. A few weeks earlier, I had announced that I was planting a church in Portland, and had been asked by the pastor to teach this week.

I taught on Luke 9:57-62. The title of my message was, "There Is No Such Thing as a But-First." I was giving up everything to follow God, and so I thought this was a perfect example of a message I could teach from my own life.

I wasn't concerned about money. I didn't raise money for the church plant and didn't ask Cornerstone Church for ongoing funding. I was taking a huge step of faith in this area. I didn't know how we were going to make it, but that didn't stop us. We were going, trusting God as we followed His lead.

It was very hard to move to a place where my wife's mother wasn't going to be able to travel (due to her cancer, as I mentioned earlier). But we were convinced we were to follow ... today. So we did.

I had my house up for sale and was set to leave. I taught this message, so I thought, from the overflow of my life, and I felt like

I could teach this with a decent amount of authority since I was literally embracing it personally.

But I had a "but first" that I didn't even recognize.

My house was on the market. I was saying that we were going "as soon as it sells." And if I'm totally honest, I felt like this was pretty radical. The problem was, I was essentially saying, "I will follow You, Lord, but first let me sell the house."

Oops.

It was after teaching this message that a friend pointed out this reality in my life. I couldn't believe I had missed that! But then again, it shouldn't surprise me. I'm certainly not above missing these types of things. We are all susceptible.

It was at this point that I spoke with a few of the elders and asked them to set a date for me. I wanted to finish well in my current position and transition things well. That was going to take some time, so they recommended that I leave in April.

We were leaving in three months. The elders affirmed this timing, even though I didn't know how I could possibly afford a mortgage and the rent in a new place if the house didn't sell before we left. Houses at this time in Southern California were on the market for up to a year already. I needed to sell in less than three months.

But I couldn't be concerned about that. If I was being called to follow, it had to be God's timing, not when I felt it was safe or once I thought I had all my ducks in a row.

We think differently when we stop asking God to reveal what our future is and begin asking Him to help us, through the power of the Holy Spirit, to be obedient today.

When our thoughts are focused on faithfully embracing the call of the gospel today, our concerns for what may or may not be next month fade to the background. When I am focused and asking the Holy Spirit to help me embrace what I do know, I am rarely concerned with what I don't know. We think differently when we are focused on joining in with all that God *is* doing rather than asking Him to come alongside us in what we are trying to do.

Thinking about being obedient today causes the ambiguity of my circumstances to become much less of a concern.

Being obedient today causes me to focus less and less on trying to get to a point of comfort later.

Somehow, someway the Holy Spirit ends up teaching me more when I am seeking to embrace what I already know, offering myself to God for His holy usage today.

In Romans 12:1-2, Paul speaks to this.

We learn from this passage that our spiritual form of worship is to sacrificially present ourselves to God. This echoes the call of the gospel that demands us to deny ourselves and join in with what God *is* doing. I said it earlier, but we must remember that Christianity is not about asking God to come alongside what we are doing, but rather to join in with what He is accomplishing!

In this Romans passage, Paul is telling us not to conform to the self-centered patterns of the world we live in, but instead to have our minds transformed and renewed by the ways of God. In so doing, he says, we then "may discern what is the will of God, what is good and acceptable and perfect" (v. 2).

We often flip this around. We want God to tell us His will before we move forward sacrificially. This passage, however, tells us that the reverse is our appropriate response. We offer ourselves first, and as we do so, God will renew our minds *so that* we might understand God's will.

When we are obedient today, we seem to just come into the knowledge of God's will for our lives tomorrow. It just seems to be revealed. We come to a point where we just know. We might not fully be able to explain how or why we know, but we can confidently discern it.

This is my experience with God, and I know it is the experience of many others as well. As I took steps of faithfulness to plant

Colossae Church, I didn't have all the answers and I couldn't even explain all the ways I knew God was calling me to go to Portland, or how I knew I was supposed to plant a church.

But I knew beyond a shadow of a doubt that it was His will for me.

I guess I could point to things like my spiritual leaders affirming it or my wife being totally on board with me or that I just had a deep seated peace about it. But the bottom line is that I can't specifically point to any one thing that led me to the understanding that this was in fact God's will for me.

The only thing that is appropriate to say is that God told me.

As I moved forward, obediently seeking to follow Him, He spoke to me in a number of different ways and through a number of different means.

He didn't speak audibly, but there was no doubt it was Him confirming my calling.

I say that as an encouragement to you, because maybe, like most people, you are looking for that one thing to affirm something. But don't you think it's pretty tough to recognize that thing when you don't even know what you are looking for? If you don't know what you are waiting for, then how will you know when you see it?

Won't you constantly be second-guessing whether *that* was *it*?

In my personal experience, and with most if not all those I know who have taken steps of faith, I can't point to only one thing that led me to confirmation. People taking steps of faith seek to be obedient in the present day; and as they do, they are somehow able to discern what God's will is for the next step.

I know it can be frustrating not to be able to apply a formula to all of this. But if there is a formula, it seems like it would be to obediently embrace what we do know, offering ourselves today and then trusting God to somehow show us what His will is for us as we do so. As we focus on today, the frustration of tomorrow seems to subside. We become far less concerned about it.

Another way of saying that is if you can focus on being obedient today, you will become more content with where you are today.

We trust we will know when He is moving us on to something else. But until we know He is leading us in a different direction, we remain contentedly committed to following Him today, and we do so by the help and power of His Spirit.

Different Questions, Different Concerns

When I began thinking of moving to Portland, I learned that having a mindset of being obedient today led me to ask a different set of questions than ever before. I took a scouting trip to check out the Portland area. I had never spent much time there, but every time I thought about planting a church, Portland was the place that came to mind. Not sure why, it just was.

So, my first step was to come to Portland to see what God would do or say. I didn't have any expectations, but since it was constantly on my mind, I at least had to come and check it off the list of possibilities. While I was there driving around, I found myself asking an entirely different set of questions than I was ever taught to ask.

My experience up to this point in my life had mostly been about watching people wait for God to show them if they were supposed to do something or not. The interesting thing with this approach is that I found a lot of people never finding that thing that proved it to them.

As I drove around the Portland metro area praying during that week, I didn't find myself asking God to prove to me I was supposed to move there. I wasn't asking Him to "show" me if this was the place I should go. I wasn't even asking Him to give me a peace—although I don't think that's wrong to pray for.

Instead, I was asking, Why *wouldn't* I come?

I was wondering what those things were that would hold me back from following God in obedience. I was sifting through my heart, trying to figure out why I wouldn't take this step of faith. I was trying to bring to surface all those things that would hold me back from taking a step of faith.

Rather than listing out the pros and cons, I was trying to see how my flesh would hold me back.

Past experiences in my life had led me to be more and more in tune with the power of my own counsels, and I had learned to decipher those from the voice of the Holy Spirit—or at least I had gotten better at doing that.

Often I find that people who are hindered from moving forward in steps of faith and obedience are asking God to give them some sort of sign before they move forward. Because of this, too often they don't take any steps at all. While they are waiting, their fears of the unknown seem to always scream louder than the Holy Spirit speaks.

Because of the counsel of fear within them, they are left wondering what's next. They're waiting for God to show up in a burning bush experience . . , so they know *for sure* it's Him speaking. When we ask God to show us if we are supposed to do something, we are looking for something external to prove it's right.

But by asking a different set of questions, we begin looking for different things and, I would argue, often landing in a different place. It's a place where we take steps of faith, not shrinking back or hesitating because of fear. The Holy Spirit leads versus our fleshly desires.

I realized the only reasons I wouldn't move to Portland were based in fear of everything I didn't yet know. I was afraid of what may or may not be. I didn't know how we would pay for the move. I didn't know if people would come and help. I didn't know how we would work out medical insurance. I didn't know where we would live. I didn't know how it would affect my relationship with my in-laws, whom I dearly love.

Focusing on these unknowns would have led me to operate from fear, not faith. Instead, I needed to operate from faith in what I knew to be true. What I was confident the Holy Spirit would remind me of and has already called me to today. I had to muffle the counsel of fear if I was going to move faithfully forward in tune with the Holy Spirit.

The bottom line is that all the reasons for why I wouldn't move to Portland were based on my own fears to protect myself. When I held all those fears and unknowns up to the call of the gospel, I realized they were not valid reasons to not follow. When our feelings are based on fear, we must cancel them out as invalid. The Holy Spirit does not lead us to operate from fear, but from faith. The hallmarks of following by faith are trust, dependence on God, and obedience today. We focus on the right things and trust God with taking care of us (see Matt. 6:25-34).

The Nonexistent Magic Formula

When reading a book like this there are always questions left unanswered and, if we are honest, we are all looking for concrete answers we can universally apply to all of our questions and circumstances. Writing a book like this is somewhat dangerous, because most people will have some question I cannot or do not answer. For that they will write a negative review on Amazon or some other website.

But the truth is, there is no magic formula. There are few concrete answers that can be universally applied in this context. Those that can be applied I have tried to offer, starting with remembering what Jesus has already taught.

But it's the desire for concrete answers that leads us to make following the Holy Spirit's direction much more difficult than it needs to be. We don't like any sort of mystery; and thus we pursue the A + B = C type of answers.

So here is how I will leave you. Here is the bottom line of all I will say in the context of a book on this issue. Here is what I know for sure:

When we, as God's people, collectively take the Scriptures seriously and

    seek to obey the things we already know we are called to do and

    are motivated by our love for God and people,

        we become more concerned about the gospel becoming known and embraced than we are about our own comforts and expectations being met.

We operate from faith versus fear.

We offer ourselves sacrificially to God today.

We engage with the people of the world because we desperately want them to know the person of Jesus.

We join a gospel-centered community of people who will build us up toward these ends.

We depend on God to meet our basic needs and reveal what His will is for us as we do so . . .

        and we all experience the Holy Spirit doing *amazing* things in and through us!

In Luke 12:8-12, Jesus tells His disciples that because of their faithfulness they will be brought before the authorities. Their obedience to the call of Jesus was going to lead them in front of people who could potentially condemn them. But Jesus tells them that in that very moment, the Holy Spirit will teach them, right then and there, and give them the very words to speak.

I sincerely hope you see that their obedience preceded the Holy Spirit's revealing what they should say. They did what they were supposed to do, what they already knew they were called to do; and then when they needed Him, the Holy Spirit would show up.

Far too many people are waiting for the Holy Spirit to show up without first taking the steps of obedience. Far too many people are waiting to feel His presence without first remembering what has already been taught. They want the Holy Spirit to show up despite their lack of obedience.

He just doesn't work like that. If you want to experience the power of the Holy Spirit in your life, you must first step out in obedience. Offer yourself as a living sacrifice today. Seek His kingdom and righteousness now.

When we collectively focus on embracing what we do know, we experience the joy of being a part of great things. When we collectively focus on embracing what we do know, we're not as concerned about what we don't know. And when the time comes for us to move on to something or somewhere else . . . we will know that too. It will be clear in that moment. You might not be able to point to a formula or even to one thing that absolutely confirms it, but you will know in the deepest part of your being what you are supposed to do.

For now, all you need to do is ask the Holy Spirit to remind you of all that Jesus has already taught, and help you embrace those things. This is not easy for any of us, which is why we all need our Helper, Counselor and Comforter.

And, again, this is why I say with complete confidence that we are *better off without Jesus.*

Every single Christian on earth is in desperate need of the Holy Spirit. Thank God, He is in all places at any given time.

REFLECTION QUESTIONS

1. How has wanting to hear God speak simply been a figure of speech in your life up to this point?

2. Which guy can you relate to the most in Luke 9:57-62?

3. How will Romans 12:1-2 affect your prayer life?

4. How has this chapter practically impacted your understanding of hearing God speak?

CHUCK BOMAR

Visit ChuckBomar.com to find Chuck's:

blog
speaking schedule
booking information

Follow him on Twitter:
twitter.com/chuckbomar

Find him on Facebook:
www.facebook.com/chuckbomar

Other ministries Chuck is a part of:
www.ColossaeChurch.org
www.CollegeLeader.org
www.iampeople.org